PhDONE

PhDONE

A PROFESSIONAL DISSERTATION EDITOR'S GUIDE TO WRITING YOUR DOCTORAL THESIS AND EARNING YOUR PHD

BY
DR. ALLEN RODA
CEO and Editor-in-Chief
DISSERTATION EDITOR

DR. LAUREN SAUNDERS,
VP of Editing and Research,
DISSERTATION EDITOR

with **KEVIN ANDERSON**

Skyhorse Publishing

Skyhorse Publishing books may be purchased in bulk at special discounts for sales promotion, corporate gifts, fund-raising, or educational purposes. Special editions can also be created to specifications. For details, contact the Special Sales Department, Skyhorse Publishing, 307 West 36th Street, 11th Floor, New York, NY 10018 or info@skyhorsepublishing.com.

Skyhorse® and Skyhorse Publishing® are registered trademarks of Skyhorse Publishing, Inc.®, a Delaware corporation.

Visit our website at www.skyhorsepublishing.com.

10 9 8 7 6 5 4 3 2 1

Library of Congress Cataloging-in-Publication Data is available on file.

Cover design by David Ter-Avanesyan
Cover photo credit Shutterstock

ISBN: 978-1-5107-7853-5
Ebook ISBN: 978-1-5107-7865-8

Printed in the United States of America

Contents

Preface

People often ask me how and why I launched a service to help doctoral students through their dissertation writing process. The fact is that it was never my intention, initially, and I really didn't know much about the dissertation process at all.

While completing my master's at Harvard, intending to continue on through my PhD, I started a small tutoring and academic consultation service. Naturally, I hired many of my Harvard colleagues, most of whom had just finished or were in the process of completing their dissertations. Of all the inquiries we received, none were more frequent or desperate than those from PhD students—and these queries came in from all over the United States and Canada. With so many overloaded advisors, the rise in online doctoral programs (many of which offer very little guidance to their students, while requiring flawless style formatting and rigorous statistical analysis), and the general stress and pressure that comes with writing a dissertation, it became very clear very early that people needed help. And not just any help, but help from experts who had advised PhD students before and, importantly, understood exactly what they were going through. So, in 2014, Dissertation Editor—a company whose entire staff had undergone and successfully completed the PhD process—was launched to serve this need.

We've now worked with thousands of PhD students, across a wide range of academic fields and from all types of academic institutions. In many cases, doctoral students need much more support than they can access. Even in the best cases, where a dissertation writer has a great committee, a supportive advisor, a collaborative cohort, and understanding family and friends, the process of completing a doctoral degree is tremendously difficult. To meet the need for this writing support, we've made it our mission to meet the writer exactly where they are in the dissertation process and tailor our services to the areas with which they most need assistance.

Most of the needs and pain points we've encountered over the years are addressed in this book, including coaching writers on topic selection and outlining; providing research assistance support for literature reviews; running statistical analyses; providing feedback on the flow and argument of results and discussion sections; editing and proofreading; citation support; tables and figures; manuscript formatting; and defense preparation. While the process and individual needs may look different for each student, most PhD candidates struggle with a similar range of issues. Even when comparing wildly different topics, the dissertation itself has many of the same goals and requirements. When writers look at the dissertation as a collection of specific, clear-cut parts rather than a massive project, it's much easier to progress toward completion.

In serving our clients' editorial and statistical needs, we've heard countless candid reflections on a range of challenges that go beyond the dissertation paper but have a direct impact on successfully writing it. Work-life balance, departmental politics, and advisor relationships are just a few of the many additional challenges PhD candidates face. While people tend to feel that they're the only ones struggling with these types of issues, we hear these stories time and again and feel it's important to share anecdotes that will help dissertation writers learn from both the mistakes and triumphs of others—and hopefully feel less alone.

The dissertation process has always been difficult. Changes to higher education and the world in general have made parts of it even more challenging. The student-as-consumer model many universities have adopted means that requiring students to take the same dissertation module more than once can benefit the institution financially. To make things worse, the trend of hiring for adjunct positions instead of tenure-track jobs has increased the workload of many dissertation supervisors—meaning that they often have less time to shepherd their advisees through the process. The rise of AI makes research, plagiarism, and questions of intellectual property and authorship increasingly complicated. The uptick in remote work and asynchronous learning post-pandemic can increase the sense of isolation a PhD candidate already experiences. Despite these hurdles, we know from our vast experience in working with all kinds of doctoral students from across the continent, that, with a little support, direction, and guidance, all students can complete their dissertation and earn their much-deserved degree. Not everyone can afford a professional tutor or editor to help them, but most can afford this book—a book we hope helps thousands more students graduate and be *PhDone.*

—Kevin Anderson, MA

Introduction

Allen had a summer internship while he was in graduate school at NYU. His boss at the time was approaching retirement at the end of a successful 35-year career. And yet, he still thought often about how much he regretted the fact that he was ABD (all but dissertation) in his graduate program. You can finish your coursework with flying colors, but you can't be *PhDone* until your dissertation has been approved. The Director of Graduate Studies in Lauren's English Department at the University of Denver famously told all her students: "There are only two types of dissertations—the ones that are done and the ones that aren't." Both of these experiences illustrate a key piece of knowledge we've learned over the years and continue to share with the thousands of doctoral students we've worked with at our company, Dissertation Editor: a dissertation can never be perfect, and the drive for perfection can be a major hindrance to completion; however, once your dissertation has been submitted and approved, it can be done. Writing a dissertation is an arduous task. It is a rite of passage from student to scholar, and a major life event for those who begin this journey. While it can, at times, feel daunting and never-ending, knowing what to expect and breaking the dissertation journey down into clear, manageable steps can help you to even enjoy the process (at least as much as possible) and, most importantly, complete it.

A dissertation is an important and unique endeavor that all would-be PhDs are required to produce. And, for the rest of your academic career, your dissertation will likely function as the key piece of proof that you have met the core requirement of obtaining a doctoral degree: contributing something original to your field of study. Whether based on scientific experiments, social science study, the production of artistic work, or analysis of existing texts, your dissertation is a written document that shows off the new thing you've discovered.

What if you've discovered something critical to your field but don't know how to put it into words? If that's the case, you're in very good company. Even for the very few dissertation writers who have already produced an extended piece of writing (an undergraduate capstone paper, master's thesis, or even a novel), the genre of the doctoral dissertation is also completely new to them. Not to mention that it must be written while navigating the many challenges of graduate study and, of course, while continuing to live your life, pay the bills, take care of the kids, maintain your relationships, and care for your mental and physical health, etc., etc. No matter the challenges, the dissertation must be completed before you walk across a stage in an objectively outrageous but somehow incredibly distinguished outfit called "regalia" or hear your name called via videoconferencing software then receive an embossed piece of paper in the mail 6–8 weeks later. Either way, a dissertation must be finished and approved before you can ask your friends, family, and eyebrow waxer to refer to you as "doctor."

Finishing a dissertation is the Mount Everest of academic achievement. Like many great but difficult things in life, the journey involved is as key as the completed product. It is our hope that the tools and anecdotes in this book will help you find ways to enjoy the process and achieve it in a reasonable amount of time. Even if a dissertation is a means to the end of achieving a doctoral degree, in our opinion it's a worthwhile endeavor in its own right. Even if you subsequently decide to enter a field outside of academia, and only your committee, editor, you, and (maybe) a few close friends or family members ever read your dissertation, it is *still* proof that you have added to existing knowledge, and that is something worth celebrating (or giving pride of place on your bookshelf). Better yet, as discussed in detail later in this book, every dissertation is worth sharing with the world in the form of a book, article, or other medium.

From our experience helping thousands of students complete their dissertations, there are two keys to navigating the challenge of writing a dissertation. First, remember your main goal in dissertation writing is *completion.* If you remember that perfection is not obtainable, but that you are nonetheless in the process of contributing to human knowledge, that can make the journey feel achievable and enjoyable. Focusing on completion can help you avoid traps like research rabbit holes, unnecessary changes of direction, trying to write exhaustively on your subject, and interminable tinkering long past the point of completion.

This leads to our second, and more tangible, key to dissertation completion success. This is preparing for the process, including the obstacles you might encounter as you work. Challenges are inevitable, but if you know what to expect and prepare for the issues that commonly arise, they won't become stumbling blocks. Preparing for the steps in the process and the obstacles you might encounter will allow you to move continually forward through the process rather than getting stuck.

We've met with countless students who have written 20-, 30-, or 40-page chapters only to have their dissertation director tell them nothing was salvageable—they would have to delete all their work and start from ground zero. While avoiding that situation in the first place is of course the goal, what is *much* more important is your reaction and the next steps should an obstacle like that present itself.

Potential obstacles to completing a dissertation come in external and internal forms. As you read this book, you will be able to prepare for the external challenges that can add extra stress, like finding an outside committee member or preparing for the defense. You will also have the space to predict internal obstacles that might come up. Perhaps you have always had a difficult time switching off from work and closing your computer at night. What about finding ways to write when you just emotionally can't handle more dissertating? If you anticipate that these sorts of things will occur during your dissertation (they will), you can develop strategies in advance to overcome internal issues. Both external and internal obstacles are inevitable, but with preparation, you can ensure that you are able to navigate the challenges that come up and can prevent behaviors that amplify the inherent difficulty of writing a dissertation. As dissertation writers, we have enough to contend with without getting in our own way as well.

That's where this book comes in. Having worked with countless students struggling with their dissertations over the years, we discovered common themes in the various challenges they have faced. Out of those experiences, we developed this guide for students, which contains both practical advice for breaking down the dissertation process and real-life examples of the obstacles dissertation writers encounter (as well as those obstacles they create for themselves). While the names have been changed, the stories in the pages that follow are from real dissertation writers who have either overcome or succumbed to the challenges you are about to face as you undertake the dissertation writing process. Some of these stories function as cautionary tales—what *not* to do. Some work as examples of strategies to emulate, and others are drifting somewhere in the limbo between what to do and what not to do. However, all of them are designed to allow you to benefit from the wisdom of those who have already been through the dissertorial fire.

Chapter 1 covers what your dissertation entails, recommendations for how to choose a topic, and an overview of the process. Chapter 2 turns to the topic of work-life balance, including treating your dissertation as a job, setting up your space and schedule for success, and navigating your relationships during the process. Chapter 3 addresses dissertation committees and how to navigate the weird waters of the advisor-advisee relationship. Chapter 4 provides writing tips and resources that will give you the foundation for doing the hard but rewarding work of dissertation writing.

Next, let's shift toward unpacking the nuts and bolts of the dissertation. What is it? What are its component parts? Chapter 5 provides the information you'll need to start the dissertation, including organizational structures, abstract, introduction, and the research/literature review process. Chapter 6, on methodology, research, and results, discusses how to develop research questions, conduct research, obtain IRB approval, and write the results and conclusion. Chapter 7 addresses the process of finishing your dissertation, including revision and editing, dissertation defense, and final submission. Chapter 8 considers next steps: converting your dissertation into a book or article and packaging your doctoral skills in a resume or in a cover letter.

CHAPTER 1

First Things First: What Is a Dissertation Anyway?

Simply put, your dissertation is the written representation of the unique contribution to knowledge you've achieved throughout your research process. Common across all areas of study, one of the main things receiving a doctorate means is that you haven't only absorbed existing knowledge in your field, but have also added something to it. Congratulations: You're in the process of contributing to human knowledge! In the humanities, this might mean that you've looked at an existing document in a way that no one has before, and your dissertation describes how and why you did so, and what important elements you found. In research-based courses of study, dissertations report the results of studies or experiments no one had ever conducted before you came along.

In a more practical sense, the dissertation is the key milestone you must meet before being awarded a doctoral degree. Most PhD programs in the United States comprise coursework during which you must take certain classes and meet certain requirements (i.e., a methodology class or a language competency exam), comprehensive exams, and the dissertation. Some programs, and especially doctoral degrees obtained abroad, often omit the coursework and sometimes the exams entirely, and treat the dissertation as the only tangible metric for awarding the terminal degree. In any case, the dissertation is the final and most significant piece of work anyone hoping to obtain a doctoral degree must accomplish.

Your dissertation is crucial to your job prospects within academia. First, your dissertation is your most specific qualification as to the aspect of your field in which you are an expert. It determines which job postings and grants you're eligible to apply for. Second, you may have heard the slightly melodramatic but fairly accurate phrase: "publish or perish." The most important element that differentiates candidates in an academic job search, particularly for tenure-line appointments, is their publication record. Publications are an essential requirement for entry into a tenure-track job in academia. Later in this book, we address the topic of turning your dissertation into a book and/or article in detail, but before beginning the dissertation and during the writing process, it's something to keep in mind. If you're able to turn your PhD dissertation into a scholarly monograph and place it with a reputable press, or to have one or more articles based on your dissertation accepted for publication with top journals, you're much more likely to have success in the academic job market.

Even if you're unsure whether you'd like to stay in academia after completing your degree, your dissertation can still help you obtain a role outside of your academic field. Rather than targeting university presses and scholarly journals, you might consider converting your dissertation into a book for the consumer market or self-publishing it. Rather than academic articles, it might turn into Op-Ed pieces or a series of posts for your professional blog. Outside of the document itself, the process of completing it is, *in itself,* something that can give a job candidate an edge in many fields. Knowing how to conduct original research and achieve something of a dissertation's magnitude is appealing to many employers, and certainly has a place in your resume, cover letter, and interview for any role you decide to seek.

Dissertation Process Overview

All these topics will be covered in more detail in the next section of this book, but this section provides a brief overview of the general steps included in the dissertation process.

Background Research and Topic Selection

Selecting a topic is one of the first and most important steps in the dissertation journey. Topic selection requires thorough background research in your field to ensure that you've got an angle that hasn't been addressed—or, at least, hasn't been addressed well or hasn't been addressed recently and could be revisited with a new perspective. Don't get dismayed when you discover unlimited resources on the topic that you want to write about. Remember that a heavily covered topic can still have an original angle if you apply it to the specific needs and circumstances of your region. You could also apply an old idea/theory to a new text or a new initiative.

The bulk of your background research will be on the specific topics, theoretical/or conceptual frameworks, and methodological choices you're in the process of selecting. Research librarians can be a particularly great resource for this phase of the process. And, best of all, their services are free. You can either go to the library or go to your library's web page to get professional assistance. Even a 15-minute session could help you uncover search strategies and resources that prove vital to your project.

Background research also extends to the detective work you might do on your prospective advisor; for example, you might find yourself reading books and articles prospective advisors and committee members have authored or provided oversight for as committee members. Even if they don't quite relate to your field, they might provide insight into whose methodologies and qualities as an academic and researcher best align with your own. This will help you see, in advance, which aspects of their work you're interested in emulating and potential points of disconnect or contention between your writing style and theirs.

Finally, you'll want to read up on your university's dissertation process and requirements. It's time to dust off your graduate student handbook and make sure you know which forms need to be submitted when and to whom, and which requirements need to be met to keep the process going forward. Importantly, don't trust your advisor to keep you on track with institutional bureaucracies. The graduate student handbook may not be on their personal reading list or may have changed since their last advisee completed their degree.

Submitting the Prospectus and/or Proposal

The next step in the process is submitting a dissertation prospectus and/or dissertation proposal. Usually, the prospectus provides a summary, literature review, and chapter breakdown, as well as clearly defining the significance of your research. A dissertation proposal tends to be much longer, comprising the first three chapters of a five-chapter dissertation (introduction, literature review, and methodology). Your institution may require either or both, so be sure to check your graduate student handbook. In either case, this is the stage in the process during which you'll likely complete your literature review (or at least a portion of it), refine your hypotheses/research questions, and decide on your theoretical/conceptual framework and methodology.

Keep in mind that this process can feel like a difficult hurdle to overcome, and it can include a lot of back-and-forth discussions with your advisor. As an example, when Jo Ann began researching her dissertation topic, she wanted to write about informatics. But her advisor realized that Jo Ann was more enamored with the future-sounding term "informatics" than she was committed to the topic. With help from her advisor, Jo Ann was able to settle on a topic that was more in her—and her advisor's—expertise.

By the end of the proposal process, you might feel as if you've written 27 different versions of each of your research questions with only infinitesimal differences between them. However, the proposal is crucial and should be considered the foundation and framework of the whole study. The more thoroughly you complete it, the easier the next stages of the process will be. The slight exception to this statement is the introduction. Never expect the first draft of your introduction to be the final version. Almost all dissertation writers substantially revise, or even totally rewrite, their introduction chapter after the rest of their dissertation is complete. When starting out, you'll write the introduction for the dissertation you intend to write, but once you've finished, you'll go back and rewrite the introduction for the dissertation you actually wrote.

Conducting Your Research

Remember that well-thought-out and detailed framework you established in your proposal: that beautifully articulated road map for the research process you painstakingly revised and obtained approval on? Now, it's time to follow it. Interview your participants, complete your survey, conduct your experiment, analyze your texts, observe your subjects, etc.—this is the part where you make the aforementioned contribution to knowledge. It's difficult, yes, but for many, this is the most fun part. It's where you get to buckle down and do the work that made you want to start a PhD program in the first place.

Analyzing Your Results and Their Significance

Depending on your field, the analysis process can involve running various statistical tests (discussed in the next section); reviewing the conclusions of your textual, historical, or ethnographic analysis; or defining codes and themes based on qualitative analysis. You'll consider how your results compare to those of previous studies (particularly those included in your literature review), what future research and real-world implications they have, and how they were expected or surprising. This is the part where you 1.) Figure out what your results are, create tables and figures to represent them, and write your results chapter and 2.) Figure out what your results mean, and why they are important, and write your discussion chapter.

Revising Your Dissertation

Great! You finished your dissertation, so now you just hand it in, and they hand you your degree, right? Well, not just yet. First, you will get several rounds of feedback from your advisor and committee members on various parts of your dissertation and the whole document and make changes that range from global to minute.

For example, Tatiana, a doctoral candidate in art history at UC Berkeley, felt relieved to turn her manuscript in to her advisor after a focused year of writing. She'd challenged herself to write at least a half page every weekday of the year and was ready to move on to new challenges. While waiting to hear back from her advisor about the manuscript, she progressed to the second round of interviews for a tenure-track position with a private university. A week later, when she read her advisor's email, she wasn't sure whether to cry or scream (she did a little of both). The note read: "I'm sorry, but your manuscript is not ready to defend. You are going to have to delete and rewrite almost all of it." Unfortunately, Tatiana's advisor was on sabbatical for most of the dissertation writing process and hadn't taken more than a glancing look at any of the chapters along the way. Tatiana took a day to steel herself to the reality of having to rewrite her dissertation. She knew that this project would take another year—maybe more. But her advisor (who felt and was partially responsible for the problem) worked with her and ultimately championed Tatiana's work and celebrated with her when she successfully defended 15 months later.

Remember that revision is an expected part of the process. Account for it and make sure you have enough time to do it justice. It's best to work from the biggest changes required (ideas, argumentation, and organization), before delving too deeply into the specifics (e.g., grammar, spelling, formatting, references).

Defending Your Dissertation

When you have a completed draft, you'll submit it to your advisor and committee, and schedule your defense. You'll prepare a presentation and spend a few hours fielding questions about your dissertation from those people who (other than you) know your work best. In most instances, you'll know the result before you walk out of the room, and this is often the first time someone will address you as "Doctor" and congratulate you on your achievement. While even thinking about the defense can be stressful, keep in mind that your advisor will not let you progress to this stage until they know you are ready for it.

Revising Your Dissertation (Again)

Now you're completely done and it's time to celebrate, right? Wrong again (sort of). You should celebrate your achievement, but it usually comes with a couple of conditions. Your committee will likely award the degree pending some level of revision, ranging from minor to major. You'll have to complete these within the time your university allots to ensure that you do actually receive the degree. However, passing your defense is a huge milestone that should be celebrated.

Formatting, Final Submission, and Bureaucracy

Finally, you'll likely need to make sure the manuscript formatting aligns with your university style guide and upload it to a repository like ProQuest. You'll need to decide whether to embargo the research for a period of time (ensure that it isn't publicly accessible right away if there are confidentiality concerns or other reasons to do so). If you want to turn your dissertation into a monograph, you will likely want to put an embargo in place. You'll also need to complete any other paperwork or requirements to make sure you're able to graduate (i.e., pay library fines, rent graduation regalia).

Choosing a Dissertation Topic

Often, the first formal foray into dissertation topic selection is the personal essay required on a graduate school application. The purpose of that document, as you likely already know, is to justify why you are the right person to conduct the research on your topic, and why you absolutely must do so at your target institution: "I'm interested in researching X, which I am uniquely qualified to do because of Y, and so it is only fitting that I work with Professor Z." Since then, though, you've likely completed an average of two years of coursework and refined your areas of expertise while completing your comprehensive exams. By the time you're required to decide on a dissertation topic, your initial plan may have changed completely. Or maybe Professor Z has moved on to another institution.

Requirements for timeline vary, but proposing the dissertation topic and having a prospectus approved usually come soon after the completion of coursework and/or comprehensive examinations. When it is time to decide on a topic, students often realize that they don't know where to begin. If that is the case for you, you're not alone! While some graduate students know from the outset what their dissertation topics will be, for others it requires extensive and sometimes onerous deliberation to land on a topic. Sometimes, it's a little bit of both. Lauren went through a long period of evaluating and reevaluating her dissertation topic, and for a while it felt like she had a new and completely different idea on a daily basis. Ultimately, she drew on her favorite elements of texts to teach to undergraduates, new perspectives gained in research methodologies courses, the expertise gained during comprehensive exams, and even the kernel of an idea she'd written about in her undergraduate capstone thesis for her dance degree. Finally, she gained approval from her advisor on a topic she felt both proud of and excited to write (the use of gestures/body movement in the writings of James Joyce and Virginia Woolf). Out of curiosity, Lauren dug up her graduate school application essay from a buried file of documents on her desktop and found that this newly minted topic was extremely similar to what she had proposed, then forgotten about in the almost four years that had elapsed since she'd written her personal statement. Lauren's process of indecision was a circuitous way back to where she'd started—only fleshed out with new experience and expertise. The resemblance ultimately showed her that she'd hit on the right dissertation topic.

Choose Something You Can Live With for a While

You might end up spending a very long time writing your dissertation. It is a common mistake to think that the process can be finished in a year. While it's field-specific, in general, one year would be a very quick dissertation writing process but *might* be possible. Two years is a more realistic timeline, and many doctoral candidates wander into the three- and four-year territory and beyond. But it takes most students three to four years to complete a dissertation or longer depending on what research needs to be conducted. As such, pick a topic that you think you will not lose interest in over time. Ask yourself: What are the issues and questions that I enjoy thinking about? What are the ideas that fascinate me and that I read and contemplate at length? Pick a topic that captures your interest and makes you excited, so you won't be bored within a year or two (or, worse, a month or two). Choose a topic that you love. If you feel passionate about your topic, then researching and writing about it will be a joy and a pleasure. If you choose something "just because," then writing the dissertation might feel impossible and your displeasure will show up in the text, reducing the quality of your dissertation and making it even harder to write. For example, Anna, who was working on her doctorate in Information Technology at Capella University, told us that she would stare at her screen and start to get a stomachache as she tried unsuccessfully to write about her chosen topic: telehealth. Ironically, she was getting physically sick just thinking about writing about health care. To make sure that you choose the right topic, follow your inspiration and your passion as much as possible. That will serve you in the long run.

Find Something Fresh

The most important factor to consider when choosing your dissertation topic is whether it will make a new and timely contribution to your discipline. Your topic must be something new. As academics like to say, you need to find a "gap in the literature," which means you need to discover something that hasn't been discussed yet. This doesn't necessarily mean you have to find a brand-new topic that is completely unexplored. Rather, you might identify a topic that has been *understudied* in your field or examine a topic from a new perspective or use a different theory or approach. You can also critically review the current research in your field and identify shortcomings that have left a gap in the literature, such as the generalizability of a population, small sample sizes, or method of analysis. Sometimes, it doesn't look like a gap. It might look more like an edge: something that has a little research but could use more, or something that can be improved, redesigned, or taken in a completely new direction.

Some writers, like Ash, who was studying Anthropology and Linguistics at the University of Arizona, go to great lengths to make their dissertation a groundbreaking piece of scholarship. Ash had funding to travel to Africa to study Ghanaian culture for a year, but two months into the process, she couldn't get any of the Ghanaians to open up to her. They would meet with her for an interview but rarely answer any of her questions with more than a yes or no. Her first plan wasn't working. Then, Ash happened to meet, fall in love with, and eventually marry a man from Ghana. She began to live their customs. As a result, she was able to connect with them more deeply and engage with them more effectively. Her ethnology is a rare window into a culture that Americans know little about. But you don't have to make a life change as significant as matrimony to find your research topic. Well, not as long as you enjoy reading.

As with research in general, it helps to start big and then get small. Think of the process of finding a gap in literature in terms of nesting dolls or stacking cups: start with a big, broad topic and do a lot of reading with your key search terms. When picking up books in a university library, take a walk down the aisle and see if any of the other books on that shelf near the one you were specifically looking for jump out at you. When Allen was conducting his initial doctoral research, he would typically go to the library for one book and leave with ten or fifteen. Among those additional "impulse checkouts," he found some real gems that proved to be influential in his dissertation. Look at themes that keep appearing or questions that keep popping up. You could also look at an area that seemed settled twenty years ago, but which there is now room to reevaluate given the modern cultural landscape or a recent discovery. The reference lists of peer-reviewed articles are great places to search for other relevant articles that might be of interest. Every piece of scholarly writing will provide breadcrumbs leading you to more and more.

A key part of the process is cultivating the discernment to know what is relevant and what is tangential to your topic. Casting a wide net at the beginning of that process will help you (and your committee) know that you have been comprehensive.

If you continue to pursue the leads you've gotten from other articles, eventually, you'll find that your research has become more specific. Pay attention to areas that have not been adequately pursued, but make sure you aren't pursuing a dead end either. Keep an eye out for reasons certain research leads have not been followed, and what has and hasn't yielded results. It can be helpful to pay careful attention to the conclusion sections of research articles, as these often include discussions of "areas for future research." Meta-analyses and review articles can be helpful for looking at larger swaths of information when searching for a gap in the literature.

Most importantly, consult the work you yourself have completed during your studies. Many graduate students can identify the germ of their dissertation in the term paper or final project they completed for an upper-division undergraduate course in their field. If you've already completed a master's degree, the thesis or research you completed for that degree may lead logically into your doctoral research. What aspects of your previous work remain unexplored? Which were of the most interest to you?

The Conversation in Your Discipline

Another way to figure out what topic might be new and fresh is to pay attention to the conversation in your discipline. Pay attention to the kinds of topics people are presenting at the big conferences in your field and the articles they are publishing in big journals. What topics are *not* represented? What gaps do you see in the knowledge? What unanswered questions do you have when you look at the conversation in your field? By asking yourself these questions, you can start to hone in on subjects that may be worthy of scholarly attention but have yet to be pursued.

Think Small and Specific

One of our clients, Phoebe, was enrolled in a prospectus writing course as part of her Industrial and Organizational Psychology doctorate at Grand Canyon University. She was disappointed to learn that her instructor would be Professor Xavier, a taskmaster known for forcing students to retake the prospectus course multiple times until he was satisfied that they had a workable idea. Of the other seven students in her cohort, many were already repeating the course and knew, in no uncertain terms, that this wouldn't be their last stop with Professor Xavier. When Phoebe first talked with her editor, she expressed frustration with the process, talked about her anxiety to show Professor Xavier her work, and repeatedly said she would never receive approval on her prospectus.

"Hold on, Phoebe," the editor said. "This class isn't over yet! You're going to get through this!"

"You think so?"

"Yes! What ideas do you have? What feedback have you been given?"

Phoebe, it turned out, had too many ideas. She wanted to interview business managers about their oversight of remote employees. She also wanted to interview remote employees to discuss their experience with remote management and their productivity working in a remote capacity. The solution was simple enough, and her professor had suggested as much. She needed to focus on one group. Too often, doctoral students make the mistake of thinking that multiple approaches will make their project easier to complete since there will be more to write about. But adding lots of approaches obscures a project's focus. A bloated project is a confusing project.

Phoebe was also stressed. She believed that if she didn't get her prospectus approved and, thus, pass her prospectus writing class, her PhD dreams would wither. Several times during her first conversation with her editor, Phoebe expressed how stressed she was over the class. And the stress from Professor Xavier's track record was keeping Phoebe from hearing the good advice that her professor was giving her. Her editor recommended that she recontextualize her study in terms of a managerial pandemic response. She could ask remote managers about their experience during the COVID-19 health crisis. And she agreed that she should remove the employees from the study. When Professor Xavier saw Phoebe's revised prospectus, he praised it. She'd heard his critique and had revised accordingly. As it turned out, Phoebe was one of only two students that Professor Xavier passed that semester.

The right dissertation topic should be precise. Like Phoebe, you may have to cut loose some ideas that you are excited about to get to a manageable project. While a dissertation is an enormous undertaking, dissertation topics need to be surprisingly narrow. You might initially set out to write a dissertation about a rather broad topic with dozens of potential subtopics, lots of questions, and no single issue around which you can build a concise argument. If this is the case, you will likely find you will need to narrow it down. The process of narrowing down your ideas will also help you refine specific hypotheses, questions, and arguments. This will help you focus your dissertation and ultimately make it easier to write and more compelling to read. The narrower you can go while identifying your topic, the better. There is always room for expansion later in the process and expanding a topic is generally easier than narrowing it down.

In research-based qualitative or quantitative dissertations, one way to narrow down your topic is to limit the research to a specific time frame or geographic location. For example, Kevon, an EdD candidate at Baylor, found that no one had studied the effect of intergenerational relationships on educational performance in his region. Even though he found similar studies, he realized that he could serve his local educational community by recontextualizing preexisting studies. He was right. The principals that he approached to participate in his study were excited about the ramifications of his study on their students.

Another way to narrow down your topic is to focus on a particular demographic population at the exclusion of others. In the humanities, this might look like zeroing in on a very small subtopic of your broader research area or bringing two small subtopics that haven't been compared before into conversation with each other. There are countless ways to narrow down your topic, and the more specific you can get at the beginning, the better off you'll be in the long run.

Consider Your Goals and Consider the Market

When Allen was choosing his dissertation topic at NYU, he received all kinds of different advice. Some of his tenured professors told him that the most important thing was to choose a topic that he would be happy with and would enjoy thinking about for the next few years. Other students in the cohorts closer to finishing their dissertations advised him to think ahead to the academic job market. They suggested that Allen look at what kind of research was getting published in the ethnomusicology field and which young scholars were getting jobs, and then pick a topic in line with those trends. Given the precarious nature of the academic job market, this sounds like very practical advice. It can be difficult, however, to predict which research topics will be hot and marketable a few years down the road when you're finally looking for work. Too often, the academic buzz-words of today get little more than eye rolls tomorrow.

Our advice is to focus on finding a topic that suits you well while keeping your professional goals in mind. Publications count for a lot on the academic job hunt, so you definitely want to choose a dissertation topic that you think could easily result in an article or two. But don't sacrifice your interests and passions in pursuit of a dissertation topic that you think will guarantee you a job, because it's all but impossible to predict what that topic will be. Furthermore, if you aren't passionate about your topic, that lack of enthusiasm will come through in your conference presentations and job interviews. You won't be able to inspire an audience if you aren't inspired.

If you aren't pursuing a PhD with an academic job in mind, then it is even more important that the topic be something useful for advancing your career. Thinking beyond the dissertation to the book you will publish after the work is completed is a good way to think about how you'll establish yourself as a thought leader in your field. How will the authorship of this book result in launching your new consultancy? What kinds of doors will open for you when you are not only a PhD, but have published a book on *this* particular topic? Ideally, that topic will be the passionate inspiration that brought you into the program in the first place; however, at the stage of choosing a topic, it's worth taking your career goals into consideration.

A colleague of Lauren's, Rebecca, was working on a dissertation about *Beowulf* but wasn't sure she wanted to pursue a career as a medievalist working inside academia. Some dissertations, Rebecca realized, lend themselves much more naturally to a transition to working outside of academia than becoming an expert on a poem written in Old English. However, Rebecca was passionate about her research and determined to make the dissertation process both align with this passion *and* advance her future career goals.

In conversation with colleagues and friends, Rebecca realized that her favorite part of academia was teaching undergraduates. She liked helping the next generation of readers get excited about texts that, at first glance, seemed totally inaccessible. Rebecca set about making her dissertation align with this goal by exploring the realm of digital humanities. As part of the dissertation process, Rebecca created a website where readers could instantly translate old English terms, overlayed over the text itself, and access images and video clips showing how Beowulf had been represented in art over time. The last chapter of Rebecca's dissertation addressed how readers from different socioeconomic backgrounds and age groups responded to the website. In the end, Rebecca's dissertation was strong enough to lend her several interviews for tenure-track medieval literature jobs, but she ultimately decided to take a position with a nonprofit that works to help underprivileged children and teenagers access the arts.

The takeaway from Rebecca's story is that the topic selection process is the right time to envision several possible futures for your career goals and work. Which of these can work together? Which do you want to prioritize? Returning to the questions of which aspects of your work you enjoy the most, and why you wanted to undertake a doctoral degree in the first place, can be great places to start.

The next chapter turns to the topic of work-life balance, and how to fit your dissertation writing process into your life and amongst your other responsibilities. While these issues arise throughout the doctoral journey, especially once you are fully immersed in the writing process, they are especially important ones to put some thought into at the outset. In the area of work-life balance, anticipating obstacles from the beginning and implementing strategies to deal with them early on will save you a great deal of time and trouble.

CHAPTER 2

The Balancing Act:
How to Juggle Your Life
and Your Work

Ever heard someone say that it's easy to take care of a newborn baby? The joke is that while that might be true, it's extremely difficult to do *absolutely anything* else while taking care of a newborn. If you never needed to eat, sleep, or shower—let alone work or cook or clean or maintain your sanity and relationships—it would be a lot more straightforward. Neither caring for a newborn nor writing a dissertation could ever genuinely be thought of as easy. However, both of these already Herculean tasks are significantly complicated by the need to continue maintaining all other aspects of your life simultaneously.

Unhelpfully, the rest of your life doesn't automatically pause when you decide to undertake the dissertation-writing process. In fact, your other responsibilities tend to become even a little more complicated. You still have to care for your basic physical and mental needs, and the stress and strain of the dissertation process might mean that you need to attend to these even more assiduously than you did before. Bills still need to be paid, and your potentially less-than-generous graduate teaching assistant stipend might make that more difficult than usual. Kids still need to be fed, clothed, entertained, and driven to violin lessons, and having stayed up late finishing an experiment tends not to make that any easier. Perhaps most importantly, personal relationships still need to be maintained, all while navigating the fact that a dissertation can, at times, feel like an all-consuming new identity. One of our clients, Sabine, told us that she felt guilty working on her dissertation instead of playing with her one-year-old. While she knew that she was working on the degree to give her daughter a better life, she couldn't help feeling like she was missing out on the life they were presently living!

There is no perfect way or one-size-fits-all solution to deal with the work-life balance conundrum. Work-life balance is difficult at the best of times, and some of the characteristics of the dissertation writing process—flexible hours, low pay, isolation, high standards, unclear benchmarks, lack of support, imposter syndrome, and a culture of perfectionism—can exacerbate it still further. While that might feel hopeless, a key point to remember is that you can't wait for your dissertation to be completed to feel like you're living your life. Your existence doesn't pause when you enroll in graduate school and resume when you triumphantly don your regalia at graduation. Personally, Lauren would attribute her happiness during the doctoral journey to the advice she received from an undergraduate advisor when she told him she was considering applying to graduate school: "Great, but just remember that your life doesn't start when you finish your PhD. If you don't feel like you're living your life *while* you're in grad school, it's not worth it." Sounds good on paper, you might be thinking, but how? The following strategies and cautionary tales should help.

Treat Writing Your Dissertation as Your Job

For this period of your life, writing your dissertation is your job. It's almost definitely not the only job you're currently holding. You might be getting your PhD while managing household and caregiving responsibilities. You might be enrolled in a program designed for asynchronous, online degree-obtainers and writing your dissertation while working in a demanding corporate role. Even if obtaining your PhD is your primary responsibility at this point in your life, you're likely expected to teach classes, serve as a research assistant, or otherwise earn your keep at your university.

The job of writing your dissertation might not be paid very well. Heck, it might not be paid at all. You might even be shelling out tuition every semester. No matter how many jobs you hold or how well, or if you're being paid for it, it's important to hold the mindset that your dissertation is your job for a few reasons. First, thinking of it this way helps you realistically assess the time and space required for the process. You're not going to be able to write your dissertation in a few casual spare hours in the week, but rather are going to have to consider re-navigating your other responsibilities and scheduling time to complete the writing process.

Second, if you're part of any kind of family unit, thinking of your dissertation as a job—and encouraging those around you to do so as well—can help you start a conversation about redistributing shared responsibilities. For example, our client

Shira and her husband Zay had been married for ten years when she began a PhD in economics. With the youngest of their three children finally in school all day, she decided it was time to transition some of her efforts from full-time childcare and household management to return to her career passion and obtain the degree she'd coveted since her undergraduate education, enrolling in Creighton University Online. She started spending 6½ hours per day on her research, writing, and other graduate school responsibilities (the time remaining from her children's eight-hour school day after subtracting the commute to drop them off and pick them up). That 6½ hours dwindled as the reality of laundry, making dinner, housecleaning, scheduling family appointments, managing the budget, paying bills, and everything else she'd previously been responsible for piled up.

When she brought up the subject to Zay, an orthodontist, it derailed into an argument about money and their respective earnings. "It was your idea to do a PhD, and you just had to do the program with no graduate stipend." Zay told her, "I don't see why I should start cooking and cleaning too when I'm earning the money." He later apologized and they had a more productive conversation that helped them balance their home economics with the burden of Shira's work in her economics program, but it's worth remembering that domestic division of labor is a prickly and historically heteronormative and gendered question at the best of times. A PhD can exacerbate this dynamic.

When they spoke further, it came out that Zay was viewing Shira's PhD as a casual hobby and drastically underestimating the time commitment it entailed. When they started talking about the dissertation as her job and had deeper conversations about the value of the endeavor (for Shira personally and for their family), things started to shift. Zay encouraged Shira to work while he took the kids to school, and he took over several of the household responsibilities he'd never participated in before. They had to work against engrained routines and underlying assumptions about gender roles and household finances, but Zay began valuing Shira's time equally to his own, helped by the conversation about treating her dissertation writing process as her full-time job.

Take a Clear and Realistic Look at Your Existing Tendencies and Problems

The dissertation writing process can amplify anything that is already an issue in your life. Dissertation writers again and again show marked consistency in their behavior and manner of expressing themselves. Difficulties they encounter in their thesis writing faithfully mirror difficulties they encounter in other areas of life, and the strengths they draw on in doctoral pursuits are the same strengths exhibited elsewhere.

Luke was writing a dissertation on "cultural literacy and college general education curricula" to complete his EdD at University of Northern Colorado. This was the second dissertation Luke had started. All his coursework and comprehensive exams were behind him, and he had been working on the current dissertation for 3½ years. Luke was mired in endless reading and research, wanting to cover every nook and cranny of his challenging topic. He had grandiose ideas of what he should accomplish: for example, when he said he had successfully chunked his project into manageable pieces, one piece was "a brief history of general education in the United States" and another was "schemes of knowledge and classification and taxonomy."

With a strong sense of industriousness, Luke developed elaborate organizing and saving techniques for his notes and articles, including sorting and re-sorting them into plastic bags labeled with magic markers, making a file folder for each paragraph he intended to write, and renting a studio apartment for his research materials. He was highly engaged intellectually and even taped pages in the shower stall with ideas to consider while showering. The broad scope of his topic meant that he was constantly discovering new relevant items and had "a nagging, gnawing sense that 'Gee, is there something else out there?' Sometimes, as a self-disciplinary measure, I tell myself the last thing I need is another idea." When to terminate library research, an ambiguous point for all students, was especially difficult for Luke.

But Luke was slow and meticulous no matter what project he was working on. His wife, for instance, was bothered by how long it took him to build a set of shelves, including several developmental stages and extensive notes on shelf design. And Luke's hobby was Japanese gardening, a ritualized and detailed pursuit. Even when a plant was properly trimmed, he didn't plant it in his garden plot's soil but sunk each one, still in its pot, into a hole in the garden in case he decided to change its location later. His wife believed that he excused himself from his stress-filled family life by vanishing into his endless projects.

The unclear limits of the dissertation project let Luke's compulsive tendencies run rampant. The unforeseeable nature of his doctoral comprehensive exams caused him to be physically sick beforehand, and he also became very sick during a leave of absence he took to write his dissertation, requiring hospitalization, morphine, and Valium. Eighteen months after getting in touch with a dissertation coach, he had not yet finished his dissertation proposal.

Luke's story is not one of the more optimistic anecdotes included in this book, but the story highlights the importance of painting as clear and unforgiving a picture as you can of your potential pitfalls and obstacles *before* beginning your dissertation writing process. It's unrealistic to think that something that has troubled you in past work, personal, or mental health arenas won't rear its head while writing a dissertation, since it can be an extremely stressful undertaking. Having experienced compulsive tendencies in the past, Luke may have found it useful to work with a counselor to develop strategies to mitigate those behaviors and their adverse effects before beginning the process. This leads to our next recommendation: use your resources.

Know All Your Resources and Use Them

Resources for mental well-being are key and are increasingly available. Most universities include at least some mental health resources in their insurance plans or at least a number of free therapy sessions for students. Online therapy avenues sometimes offer care at a fraction of the price of traditional in-person sessions, with flexibility that can make it easier to schedule and stick to sessions. Apps for meditation and exercise often offer student discounts and free trials, and you may have access to a gym membership, peer support, or other tools that may benefit your well-being through your university. We suggest getting in touch with your school's counseling and psychological services center. While the stigma surrounding necessary mental health and self-care is decreasing, many still find it difficult to identify their need for help or to seek it. However, it's worth remembering that *everyone* can benefit from therapy or counseling services, even at the best of times, and that mental health care is important preventative medicine. Dissertation writing is a stressful process, and strategies for coping can go a long way to helping you stay healthy.

Similarly, writing support can be crucial during the dissertation process, and many support options are available. A writing group can provide support, accountability, and camaraderie with members of your cohort or other graduate students at your university. If this resource doesn't exist at your school, it likely won't be difficult to find other interested individuals to join you. Such communities also abound online. University writing centers are also great tools, often providing coaching on the writing process, from brainstorming through revision.

Should I Go to the Writing Center, or Should I Hire an Editor?

It's worth highlighting the differences between the service university writing centers provide, compared to paying for professional editing services—like those a company like Dissertation Editor—provides. The main difference is that writing centers usually train their consultants not to be overly "directive." This means that your writing center consultant is more likely to engage in an open dialog with you about the most effective ways to organize your ideas, but that they're unlikely to tell you, "This sentence should go here, and this should be reworded to say—." As a writing center consultant, Lauren was always told to focus on pedagogy and "to improve the writer, not the writing." A writing center is a wonderful, and usually free, resource. Writing centers are particularly helpful for brainstorming, getting inspiration, and revising your work. What a writing center consultant is unlikely to do is take a piece of writing and correct errors *for you* at the line level.

Fixing the writing is where hiring a professional editor can be helpful. While Dissertation Editor provides consultation services to help clients with brainstorming, coaching, and research assistance, we can also do more of the fine-tuning work as well. Unlike writing center consultants, editors can correct line-level errors in grammar, punctuation, and spelling, as well as improve syntax, organization, and scholarly tone for clients. Formatting services are also a key element of professional editors' services, including creating automatically updating tables of contents and lists of tables and figures to align with university guidelines; correcting pagination, margins, and spacing; formatting reference list entries per the required academic style guide; and cross-referencing references with in-text citations.

It's a good idea to consider your budget and the value of your time when deciding whether to enlist outside help. The time and energy spent agonizing over how to create a different pagination scheme for your front matter and the body of your text might serve you better if you spend it preparing for your defense. Lauren has told each of her friends who were finishing their dissertation that she would be very angry with them if they spent time on things like university formatting or final reference checks, since she knew it would take her a fraction of the time and alleviate a great deal of unnecessary stress for them. Think about which pieces of the process might be better delegated to someone who does it for a living.

Boundaries Are Key

Students underestimate how much their love and work lives will be intertwined with their doctoral pursuits. They often don't realize that life is a system, with all its parts influencing and being influenced by each other. For example, when Barrett, a church pastor who was completing his DMin at Liberty University, told his wife he was finding it very difficult to accept his dissertation director's critiques, she wasn't surprised at all. She reminded him that he would always get angry and storm out of the room if she tried to offer him her own advice.

It's a common belief that people go through identity crises when recovering from alcoholism, and Rick was deeply involved in Alcoholics Anonymous while writing his dissertation for a clinical psychology doctorate at the University of New Mexico. He found a girlfriend named Katy in AA, and she supported him in his efforts to stay sober. However, she was not knowledgeable about academia and its pressures or about the stress of writing a dissertation. The intimacy versus isolation crisis, always a problem for a writer, cropped up as she had difficulty understanding that he really did not have weekends free. She was also upset to hear that his dissertation might take longer than predicted—a lot longer—since she had her own life to plan. After four months, she broke up with him.

Role confusion struck again when Rick accepted a job as coordinator of the High Potential Students (HPS) English program, designed for educationally disadvantaged undergraduates. "I had planned to have this nice linear program worked out and all these little variables that I hadn't considered changed," he said. The coordinator job required that Rick retrain himself as a remedial writing teacher and as a program administrator (for $100 extra a month and an impressive line on his vita). At some point, Rick understood that he "maybe should have turned down the HPS gig," and his advisor expressed concern that the HPS job splintered Rick into too many pieces. Further undermining his role stability, the graduate director lost track of Rick's status as a graduate student and sent him "a nasty letter nagging me about master's level requirements." Rick also underwent a 100 percent turnover of committee personnel that left him feeling quite insecure.

Over the summer after the breakup with Katy, Rick said, "I didn't feel much like doing anything." It was at this time that a committee member left the school and Rick's committee, citing "personal reasons." Rick didn't see a coincidence; he saw himself as a seven-year-old as his mother left him and his father. Rick wasn't sure if he could even finish his dissertation in light of all the instability. He met with one of our editors for a consultation about his literature review chapter. In response to his editor's question about what he thought about the next phase of the project, he shrugged and said, "Somebody will quit on me, or someone will die, or someone will move away."

But, by September, he reported increased ambition in his schoolwork. His quest for sobriety had inspired him to define life goals, something he had avoided before. Within six months, Rick developed a mutually supportive relationship with a young woman entering the same program at the university. This woman shared his everyday concerns, and he described her as "a diligent student," the type he was now aiming to socialize with; he showed her the ropes of the difficult program in which they were both students. He saw that he needed to surround himself with upbeat, high-achieving people instead of looking for friends among the burdened souls he met at AA.

Just like in life, healthy boundaries are key to dissertation success and happiness. First, think about your spatial boundaries. Like all remote work, dissertation writing lends itself to bleeding into every aspect of your life. While there is undoubtedly some benefit to writing on your laptop from the comfort of your bed, it's healthy to establish spatial boundaries, even if they are slight (e.g., I only work on my dissertation at my desk; the bedroom is for rest). Availing of separate spaces—like your on-campus office (if you've been assigned one), study spaces at university or public libraries, and coffee shops—can also help you separate the place you work from the place where you rest.

Similarly, creating a schedule can help you set boundaries on your time, and ensure that you don't work eighteen hours a day. While maintaining creative flexibility is ideal for some, deciding on specified writing hours is often a beneficial tool. Even treating the writing process as a nine-to-five job can help many doctoral students set healthy boundaries for themselves. At the very least, creating some time to unplug from the dissertation is key.

Boundaries in relationships are also crucial. It's useful to spend time thinking about how much talking about your dissertation is a.) Useful for you and b.) Tolerable for friends and family members. While it feels great to have those close to you take an interest in your work, and while it can be helpful to discuss your project with people outside of your field/university, when all your conversations begin and end with your dissertation, that becomes difficult for everyone. Some lucky dissertation writers have friends and family who not only take an interest in their dissertation, but actively want to help. This can be great, but it requires caution. If you let the personal relationship become too embroiled with your professional work, boundaries can be crossed and feelings hurt.

Lauren once edited a dissertation where the writer had asked his wife to read and provide commentary on it. She had some useful ideas and had put a lot of time into engaging with her partner's research and ideas. However, there were barbed and passive-aggressive comments littered throughout her feedback. On one passage that contained a few grammar and spelling errors, as well as confusing syntax, she'd written, "No offense, but I don't understand how the writing is this bad when you've been spending so much time on this." Whether offense was taken or not, Lauren felt strongly that it was intended. So, find the line between accepting help and adding a tense dynamic to an existing relationship. Remember that it's wonderful if your friend, family member, or partner is willing and able to provide auxiliary academic support, but that it is *not* their responsibility, and they are definitely *not* your editor or advisor.

The next chapter addresses advisors and committees—how to select them, and how to navigate your relationships with them once you've done so. These relationships can be wonderful or fraught, but we've never encountered anyone who has completed a PhD who doesn't have at least one story about a time when they felt stressed about their advisor. Lauren had a great relationship with her advisor and found her to be insightful and present throughout the process. Right before her dissertation defense, Lauren's advisor emailed her a definition of one of the words included in the dissertation's title. *Does she think I don't know what one of the very core elements of my dissertation means?* Lauren thought, letting her anxiety run wild. In hindsight, it was obvious that her advisor was just guiding Lauren to remember the foundation of her work and go back to basics. Advisors can at times be difficult, but the fact that PhD completion is inherently stressful can also lead to hypersensitivity, and means that these relationships too can be tricky to navigate. The recommendations in the next chapter are designed to help you preempt any issues that might arise and navigate the advisor-advisee relationship with ease.

CHAPTER 3

Picking Your Team: The Dissertation Committee and the Advisor-Advisee Relationship

The Dissertation Committee

Your dissertation committee is a team of professors who are meant to provide expertise, guidance, and mentorship as you write your dissertation. They are the audience for whom your dissertation is written. While many students like to think of their research as being relevant to a larger community, the truth is that dissertations are ultimately written for dissertation committees. After dissertations have been approved by the committees, then that same research can be rewritten into books and journal articles for the larger audiences we researchers imagine for our doctoral work. We say this up front because it is important to keep your audience in mind when undertaking any major writing project. In the case of doctoral dissertations, the audience is tremendously small and often hand-selected by you, the author.

In most cases, your dissertation committee members will be faculty whose research is similar to your own, either in topic or approach. They may be experts in the specific topic area that you are writing your dissertation about. Alternatively, they may be experts in a particular research methodology you are using. One of those committee members, typically referred to as the *chair*, fulfills the role of dissertation advisor and is the primary guide/mentor for you throughout your dissertation journey (more on that coming up).

Why a Committee?

By having multiple faculty members serve as sources of dissertation help, your dissertation will be richer. You'll be able to gather perspectives and feedback from a range of different scholars. Working with a committee is also a precautionary measure. For example, if, for some reason, your relationship with your advisor goes awry, your committee can support you and can step in, if need be. The committee also enables the university to ensure that only top-notch research gets approved. Rather than a lone professor, a team of faculty members is required to approve your dissertation. They are each staking their academic reputation on the fact that the dissertation they approve is, in fact, high-quality research, worthy of a PhD degree. The committee thus functions as a system of checks and balances to ensure that advisors are neither unjustly holding students back from finishing nor hastily pushing students whose work is unworthy of the degree through the process.

Who Chooses Your Dissertation Committee Members?

At some institutions, you will have the opportunity to choose your committee members. You'll be able to ask faculty members to join your dissertation committee. At other institutions, you may be assigned dissertation committee members. Be sure to find out early in your graduate school career whether or not it is your responsibility to assemble your committee. This information can typically be found in your graduate school handbook. If you are able to choose your committee, this may influence the selection of your dissertation topic as well as other elements of the writing process. For example, you may decide to read up on the research your committee has published, considering their arguments, the methods they have used, and their limitations/strengths before making decisions about your own project. This bit of knowledge may help you gain insight into their expectations, research interests, and the types of questions/concerns they may have about your research project.

How Should I Choose Dissertation Committee Members?

Typically, students choose their advisor first. Be sure to review the section of this book titled "Your Dissertation Advisor" (see page 45) for information about selecting and working with a dissertation advisor. Asking your advisor for suggestions for committee members is a great way to ensure that you will have a committee that gets along, or at least shares a vision for how your dissertation project should unfold.

Pay attention to the initial responses you get from professors when discussing your project. Watch for body language. If a professor hesitates or says that they're not sure they'd be the best fit, take them at their word and look elsewhere. The first professor one of our clients, Bex, asked to serve as their dissertation director said that very phrase: "I'm not sure I'd be the best fit." Bex didn't know at the time that he had just used a polite academic phrase that really meant, "Get out of my office and leave me alone forever." So, Bex asked him if he'd be willing to serve on their committee, just not as the director. His response? "No, as I said before, I don't think I'd be a good fit for this project." Here, the "as I said before" is a professional way of saying, "Are you deaf? I said no!" At the time, Bex was frustrated that the professor wasn't getting on board with the project, but in hindsight, Bex was grateful that the professor did not acquiesce and serve on their committee. He knew he wasn't a good fit and was letting Bex know it.

Seeking out scholars whose backgrounds complement that of your advisor can be a valuable strategy. If your advisor shares the same area of interest as you, but you plan on conducting research using a different methodology, then finding a committee member who has expertise in that methodology is a wise move. If you think of your dissertation as having many different aspects or components, your committee is your hand-selected team of experts who can help you develop each of those components so that your overall argument is coherent and strong.

What Should Your Dissertation Committee Do?

The degree of involvement your committee will have in your dissertation depends on the culture of your department. Sometimes, committee members provide in-depth editing. Other times, they may only be interested in reading and commenting on final drafts, or simply showing up for the defense. As you begin the doctoral-writing process, make sure to sit down with your committee members and talk about how involved they will be at each step of the process. Setting these expectations at the outset can help you avoid misunderstandings down the road.

What If Your Dissertation Committee Doesn't Get Along?

Sometimes, dissertation committees can get unruly and chaotic. Faculty members may have conflicting strong opinions or biases, and the professional relationships among your dissertation committee members may be difficult for you to navigate. Remember this: if your dissertation committee members have conflicts among each other that manifest in the way they treat you, try not to take it personally. It can be tough, but remember that if your dissertation committee members are in conflict with one another, it isn't a reflection of the quality of your work. If your committee members speak negatively about each other in front of you, be sure to maintain professionalism and politely decline to participate in any gossip or discussion that isn't pertinent to your project. Taking sides with one of your professors against another is a sure way to torpedo your project. Sometimes, dissertation committee members may disagree about the direction of your project. In those circumstances, your dissertation chair/advisor will make the final call, and you can ask them to offer an opinion or mediate.

Your Dissertation Advisor

In addition to providing you with guidance and support while developing your dissertation, your advisor is typically the first gatekeeper toward your advancement through the doctoral journey. Without your advisor's approval, you will not be able to defend your proposal to begin conducting your research. Without your advisor's approval, you cannot send your chapters out to the rest of the committee for their approval. The relationship you have with your advisor and the way in which they shepherd you through the process from topic selection to proposal, and to defense can make or break your grad school experience. The right advisor can mentor you throughout graduate school and beyond, but the wrong advisor can hamper your progress and hold you back. So, how do you pick the right dissertation advisor?

Meet Many Professors

While some doctoral programs assign you an advisor or require you to choose an advisor before you begin, others allow you to choose an advisor after you've been in the program for a while. If you're in the latter situation, take as many classes as you can with as many different faculty members as possible. Visit professors during their office hours for guidance and feedback on your coursework to get a sense of what your one-on-one relationship might be like if you selected them as your dissertation advisor. This way, you'll learn which faculty members' working styles and personalities you like. Do you want an advisor who takes a laissez-faire approach and will let you pursue your dissertation in any way you like? Or do you want someone who takes a heavier hand in guiding your work? The best way to get a good sense of what a faculty member will be like as a dissertation advisor is by working with them ahead of time. If you need to find an advisor before you begin a program, contact professors, try to meet with them at conferences, and talk to their current students so that you can find out what their working style is like.

A dissertation writer's match or mismatch with her advisor is a substantial factor in her success or delay. Be warned: it is crucial to select the right advisor. We've seen too many students get saddled with an unwieldy and adversarial committee member that effectively stonewalled their doctoral candidate, leaving them nothing to do but leave the program. Charis's advisor, Dr. Farrington, was a scholar in British Literature studies, highly recognized and accomplished in his field. Indeed, students with glowing recommendation letters in hand from Dr. Farrington often received tenure track offers. But his advice to Charis was manipulative from the beginning of their professional relationship. When Charis was invited to speak at a regional conference, Dr. Farrington told Charis in no uncertain terms that he would likely not want to write her a job recommendation letter if she presented at conferences before he gave her his blessing. Charis felt that something was off, but disregarded it. She was developing a professional rapport with the esteemed Dr. Farrington, after all! A year later, she asked Farrington to chair her dissertation committee. To her detriment, he agreed. For the next three years, Charis could never write anything that Dr. Farrington found worthy of Joycean studies and, in his words, nothing that would "Make me apt to write a recommendation letter for you." When Charis left the program, Dr. Farrington told her it was for the best.

But what exactly is a good match? Hallie's chosen advisor, Dr. Arbuthnot, seemed like an ideal match because his specialty in American literature was directly in Hallie's favorite area of study. Hallie thought this expertise would be a great help in designing and writing her research. What Hallie hadn't thought about was that Dr. Arbuthnot had a small office on a different floor than the rest of the department, the office had no window, and Dr. Arbuthnot was not on a dissertation committee for any of the other American literature students. Hallie paid no attention to these signs that Dr. Arbuthnot was an outcast among his peers, even though he was tenured and had published several well-received monographs in Hallie's chosen area. When it became clear that she was going to have difficulty recruiting committee members and that Dr. Arbuthnot was out of favor in general, Hallie regretted her decision to match only on topic area.

Carl and his advisor, Dr. Simon, were a perfect match in personality and intellect. Both loved to sit in Dr. Simon's office discussing ideas and philosophy at length. Both hated to be driven by calendar deadlines. Dr. Simon thought that deadlines and scholarly discipline were "inherited from the dysfunctional nuclear family" and said that his approach to a dissertation student was "completely laissez-faire. A friend, a colleague-scholar-friend sort of thing." This relationship was Carl's ideal, too. However, it resulted in a long, rambling process that switched directions weekly, made worse by Dr. Simon's stubborn resistance to learning the protocols ("secretarial paperwork") required by the department, college, and university. In this case, the relationship's strength was also the student's downfall.

Another faculty member, Dr. Lavrenti, described himself as an intrusive advisor: "My reputation is that my students finish. I call them, I nag them, I cajole them, I remind them." He has called advisees at 4 a.m. and said, "I'm up reading. Why aren't you up writing?" "We hold their feet to the fire down here," he said cheerfully. He has gone so far as to get one advisee thrown off a volunteer softball team so that he would spend more time writing. Though one might think that no one would choose Dr. Lavrenti as an advisor, many students do. They know that they can depend on him, and he'll supplement the self-control they may not be able to muster by themselves. Dr. Lavrenti's style has proven complementary to his students as the 100 percent pass rate among his advisees bears witness. In contrast, Dr. Simon has never had a dissertation student finish under his tutelage.

Compatible Research Interests and Methodologies

To get the advising you need to complete your dissertation successfully, you need to find someone who shares compatible research interests or methods. Your choice of dissertation topic and dissertation advisor are linked. Your advisor doesn't necessarily need to do research on the exact same topic as your dissertation, but it can be helpful if they work in a closely connected area. Alternatively, you may want to work with someone who uses methods that you want to use. For example, perhaps you want to do an ethnographic project. You may seek out a dissertation advisor who is an expert ethnographer but doesn't necessarily work with the same group of people you plan to research.

Read Their Work

The best way to find a dissertation advisor with research interests compatible with your own is to read widely in your field and identify the scholarship you like the best. You likely experienced a similar version of this step in the process before entering graduate school. You may have chosen to attend your institution because the book that was most foundational to your thoughts was authored by someone in your department. If you're considering various people in your department, read their work even if it doesn't directly relate to your own. Of course, you'll already be reading widely in your field, but this type of reading is focused more on reading texts published by your potential advisor to gain insight into how they think and work. You likely already know whether their research interests align with your own but reading their work will help you learn what they value as researchers and academics, what methodologies they employ, and what characterizes their writing style.

Will Your Dissertation Advisor Support You?

It is crucial to find an advisor who will provide the support that you need. When you are fielding potential advisors, watch out for signs that they might not be present when you need them. Do they often travel for research? Are they going to be up for tenure soon and focused on their own career? Are they close to retirement? If so, they may not be able to provide you with the one-on-one support that a doctoral candidate needs from their dissertation advisor. Again, that might not be what you need, but if it is, these are important considerations when choosing your advisor.

Talk to Students

Talk to other graduate students, both before and after you get into graduate school. If there is a professor you are interested in working with, seek out and talk to their current advisees. Graduate students can offer frank, upfront advice about a potential advisor, and warn you of any potential red flags or conflicts. Don't be afraid to ask students tough questions about their advisors. Students can tell you how long their advisor takes to read and respond to their work and whether their advisor is supportive or overly critical. These insights will be important as you make your decision.

A good advisor-advisee relationship takes two people to make it work, so good communication is key. Look for potential advisors early in the graduate school process. If you can assist a professor as a research assistant, that can function as a good "trial run" to see how you work together. Lauren had the good fortune to work with a professor who demonstrated how to schedule your way into completing a project by daily completing manageable tasks. He also related his own experiences as a student and professor, which helped Lauren understand what to expect in the job market and in the profession. What was some of his advice? "Take your time, don't make a hasty decision, and ensure you fulfill *your* responsibilities as an advisee and a postgraduate student." Expectations of the student's responsibilities are usually laid out in a university's graduate school handbook. In a worst-case scenario, your advisor will be one in name only and you will find mentoring elsewhere.

Dealing With a Difficult Advisor

In a perfect world, your dissertation advisor would always read and return emails promptly, provide unwavering support, and share expert guidance that always hits the mark. Their edits would be illuminating, clearly explained, and would propel you to the next part of your paper. Of course, our advisors are only human, and sometimes we find ourselves working with a difficult advisor. We might encounter this in the workplace as well—a challenging coworker, a difficult boss, a prickly supervisor. It's always good to know how to deal with a person like this without losing your cool or becoming derailed. I've had hundreds of conversations with students about their advisors. Here are some things to keep in mind.

Common Issues With Difficult Advisors

Advisors can be difficult for a variety of reasons. Sometimes it's an issue of personalities and work styles not meshing well. If you're wondering whether your advisor's behavior is problematic, here are some common issues that cause friction in the advisor-student relationship, alongside examples from clients of ours who have spoken to us about these issues:

- You get no response or very little response when you turn in work.

    Eleanor's advisor was absolutely great—when he actually made time to read her work. When she submitted the first full draft of her public policy dissertation to him at the beginning of August, she had visions of graduating in December. At the end of October, after several unanswered emails and empty promises, Eleanor warned him that if he didn't give her feedback by Thanksgiving, she was going to petition the University for a new advisor. He gave Eleanor feedback to one chapter on the Wednesday before Thanksgiving and finally the last of his feedback by the end of January. Eleanor's threats to change advisors may or may not have been empty. She told her editor that she's not sure what she would have done had he not finally read it. Ultimately, Eleanor graduated the following May.

- The advisor expresses frustration or seems disappointed in your work without providing any guidance or constructive feedback.

    We see this one often with many of our clients. Many advisors have too many responsibilities and simply don't have the time to go the extra mile with students who need the support. Some students who need the heavy-handed advisor end up with laissez-faire—simply because none of the faculty at their university have the bandwidth to be heavy handed. As a result, they get comments that simply say, "unclear, please explain," without any idea what is unclear or needs explaining. We've seen countless dissertations where three to five pages in, the advisor leaves a comment saying, "I refuse to read any further," often followed by an expression of frustration in the quality of the work thus far presented. Students with advisors like these are among those most likely to pursue outside help.

- The advisor doesn't get on well with other committee members and contributes to gridlock and delays.

  A statistics client of ours, Seamus, had determined in conversation with his advisor that two-way ANOVA would be the best test to use to analyze the results of his survey on burnout among different groups of nurse practitioners. We helped him run the test and he was immersed in the process of writing his results chapter, when he received a reply with belated feedback to the methodology chapter he'd sent to one of his other committee members months earlier. She insisted that ANCOVA would be preferable. Knowing this would, of course, require running a new test, as well as completely changing the results of the analysis and taking into account a covariate he and his advisor had decided not to consider, Seamus went to his advisor, who told him to "ignore her, she doesn't know what she's talking about." Predictably, this same committee member refused to approve the results chapter based on the initial analysis. It wasn't until Seamus asked his third committee member to weigh in and mediate between the others and help with a final decision that he was actually able to move forward after a great deal of stress and delay.

- Inappropriate relationships (e.g., being overly involved in a student's life or asking personal questions or favors).

  There was a professor at Alex's university who had a reputation for this. The students he advised formed a sort of clique around him. They were all intimately involved in each others' lives in a way that might have been supportive but was also seemingly problematic and prone to gossip and melodrama. That professor didn't seem to respect boundaries or would relish in pushing against them. Alex remembered having had a very awkward conversation with him while standing at the adjacent urinal after class. Nothing said crossed any official boundaries, but the interaction didn't sit well with Alex, who came to us for help interpreting vague feedback from his own advisor. He mentioned this story to his editor in a "well, it could be worse" tone, after complaining about the difficulty of parsing his own advisor's commentary on his writing.

- Questionable professional or academic behavior (plagiarism; lack of regard for ethics).

  One student, Ian, felt that his chair was presenting his ideas as if they were her own at a national conference. They'd had many candid conversations, but he was dismayed when before his dissertation was published key theoretical ideas he felt he had developed showed up in an article published by his advisor. While it is quite likely that these ideas emerged in dialogue and that the chair felt she had as much ownership to them as the student did, the fact that he felt this way about the relationship poisoned the well of trust between them, making it very difficult for Ian to move forward.

- Demeaning attitude toward student, harassment, or abusiveness in words or tone.

    One of the professors in Farah's history department absolutely terrified her. When she had to attend office hours, the advisor mocked each of her ideas and contributions to the conversation, often saying things like "what an undergraduate way of thinking about that" and "I don't understand why you were accepted into this program. It's going downhill lately." While the professor was someone Farah had initially hoped to work with, he was, after all, well respected in his field, and prolifically published on topics adjacent to Farah's, she knew that the relationship would be a disaster. Ultimately, the advisor told Farah, "You're a fool for not having my name on your dissertation," which only served to confirm to Farah that she'd made the correct choice not to ask her to serve as a committee member, and certainly not as an advisor.

If you need to create a space where you can still forge ahead with your work and maintain your sanity, consider developing clear and reasonable boundaries, both personally and with your work, and share them with your advisor. It may also be helpful to search for support and resources, outside of your advisor, such as a tutor or editor, that help you get what you need to achieve your goals. Both strategies will help you take care of yourself and progress with your work, while simultaneously trying to manage a difficult advisor.

It might also be worth identifying areas where you and your advisor agree and where you diverge. Make a list, identify the problems you're having and what you'd like to see changed, and if your advisor is willing, meet with them to discuss how these differences can be managed to create a more successful relationship. Ask your advisor if they have ideas about how to move forward or any alternative solutions.

If you find yourself struggling with any of the above issues and are unable to address them with your advisor, find a faculty member you can trust and (in a professional manner) ask how you might handle the situation. Keep any written communications you have with your advisor, document any inappropriate or abusive behavior, and seek support from fellow graduate students to help keep you on track with your work. Update your committee members on your progress and reach out to them with what you need (e.g., if you would like to start the next section of your dissertation by a certain date, let them know). This way, if any problems arise, it's clear where the problem lies.

What is the standard protocol for dealing with problematic advisors? Some schools will guide you to the department chair and others might suggest going to the ombudsman's office. The ombudsman will conduct an independent inquiry into the issue and then provide strategies to help resolve conflicts or problems. Hopefully, you will never have to experience any of these difficulties, but it's important to be prepared in case you do!

Evaluating the Nuclear Option:
Deciding Whether to Switch Advisors

When Muhammad, a doctoral candidate in mathematics at Georgia Tech, asked for feedback from his advisor, his communications were rarely reciprocated. During one of their early conversations, just after starting graduate school, Muhammad was relieved to find that his advisor seemed incredibly supportive: a collaborator and cheerleader in the process. He told Muhammad to feel free to send him any work he produced, even if it was only a few sentences at a time, and he would be happy to provide feedback on it. Muhammad did so, assiduously sending him sections of writing on a biweekly basis. He never received a reply. During their next meeting, Muhammad asked him if he had any thoughts on the work so far, to which he replied that he'd need to see a whole chapter before providing feedback would be worth his time.

Undeterred, Muhammad put his head down and completed a draft of an entire chapter, breathing a sigh of relief as he emailed it off. Three weeks later, he received feedback, the extent of which was the correction of seven punctuation errors. When he submitted the next chapter, the sparse feedback only addressed issues with APA-style in-text citations. During another in-person meeting, Muhammad asked a question about a fundamental aspect of his research design, and his advisor's answer made it clear that he hadn't yet read *any* of the material Muhammad had sent.

At this juncture, Muhammad had two choices. He could go through the laborious process of trying to change advisors, or he could maintain the relationship, but seek additional help elsewhere. When dissertation writers find themselves so at odds with an advisor that they contemplate the idea of attempting to switch, there are several key points that must be considered:

1. How damaging is the advisor's behavior? In Muhammad's case, the issue was frustrating and was affecting his workflow, but not otherwise causing undue distress. If an advisor's behavior is inappropriate or abusive, and if it's affecting your mental health or desire to complete your dissertation, your course of action may need to be different.

2. How valuable is the advisor's *name*? Is your advisor the preeminent scholar in your entire field? If so, and their behavior isn't egregious or damaging, the professional value of having worked with them *might* be enough to offset the fact that they're not providing the tangible help you need. Is another professor on your committee just as respected in the scholarly community, but much more willing to help? In that instance, it might be worth investigating your options to change advisors.

3. Can you seek support elsewhere? Are the other members of your committee much more supportive? Can you join a writing group with colleagues who review each other's work? Should you hire a dissertation coach/editor? Your other avenues for support are worth keeping in mind during this decision as well.

In the end, Muhammad decided that his advisor's reputation was going to be of significant value on the job market. He developed a closer relationship with one of the other professors on his committee, joined a group of peers, and hired an editor. With those additional support options in place, he was able to keep the relationship and association with his advisor, while still obtaining the help he needed. Most importantly, whether the nuclear advisor-switching option is best for you must be handled on a case-by-case basis, and ideally after seeking the feedback of a trusted colleague, friend, family member, therapist, or another committee member/professor in your department (though tread carefully here and be aware of the possibility that something you say could get back to your advisor).

Outside Committee Members or Readers Can Improve Your Dissertation

When you work with someone outside of your field of study, they can introduce you to ideas that may help your work become more innovative and interesting. Being able to carry out interdisciplinary research (i.e., research that engages with more than one academic field) may provide you with an advantage when you enter the academic job market. At the very least, it means that your dissertation will have a greater impact on the scholarly community, not just on academics in your field. Outside committee members can also help you learn new research strategies that will help you become a better interdisciplinary scholar and potentially introduce you to scholars beyond your field, helping you extend your academic network. Lauren's outside committee member wound up giving her a strategy for organizing her chapters that proved extremely helpful. Her advisor and other two committee members were all in the literature department and didn't recommend any changes to

Lauren's initial, and conventional, structure of dividing chapters according to the key literary texts studied: one on *Ulysses*, one on *Finnegans Wake*, one on *Between the Acts*, and one on *To the Lighthouse*. Her outside committee member, a scholar from the music department, could see thematic resonances of "musical gesture," "rhythmic gesture," etc., that none of the others had initially considered. After revising the work to be thematic rather than separated according to each literary text, Lauren's advisor and other committee members all agreed that its flow and progression of argument had significantly improved.

How to Find the Perfect Outside Committee Member or Outside Reader

In some departments, graduate students get to choose their outside committee member or outside reader. In other departments, the role may be assigned by your dissertation advisor. If you are able to choose your own outside collaborator, the best way to ensure that your relationship with your outside committee member will be beneficial is to find someone with whom you can work well. Since graduate departments are often isolated from one another, it can be difficult to get to know faculty from other parts of your university. However, there are ways to make those connections!

- <u>While you're in coursework, take classes in other departments</u>. Some programs require or allow you to take courses outside of your field. This is a great way to meet faculty and provides a chance to see how those faculty members work with graduate students.

- <u>Meet graduate students from other departments</u>. If your campus has a Graduate Students' Association or similar organization, try going to their events so that you can meet students in other departments. They may be able to offer suggestions or introduce you to their faculty members. If you know a fellow graduate student whose research interests you, find out who their advisor is. That person could be a great outside reader for you.
- <u>Attend research symposiums, talks, and events hosted by other departments</u>. This is another great way to meet faculty from outside your department and find out about their research. If you like someone's work, don't be shy about introducing yourself or following up with an email.
- <u>Ask your advisor.</u> They'll know faculty whose research may have connections to your dissertation and may be able to arrange introductions.

Developing a Good Relationship With Your Outside Committee Member

Faculty members are often quite busy, and sometimes seem inaccessible. Furthermore, many see their primary responsibility being to students in their home departments, even if they agree to serve on your dissertation committee. Talk to your outside committee member or outside reader about how involved they are willing to be in your dissertation process. Are they willing to read drafts? Are they willing to meet with you a couple of times each semester to talk about your progress or help you work through your ideas? How far in advance of a defense or exam date do they need to receive your work? As with committee members from inside your department, it is always best to work these issues out in advance to avoid misunderstanding down the line. If you're worried that your outside reader might not approve of your dissertation topic or research methods, remember that, at the end of the day, your dissertation advisor or committee chair will have the final say.

Before delving into the specific sections included in a dissertation, the next chapter provides advice to set yourself up for success in the writing process. It includes a discussion of how to lean into your unique writing style, how to think outside the box, what reference texts can be useful to read before you start writing, and how to navigate writer's block. Like the groundwork you've created by evaluating how to fit your dissertation into your life and how to cultivate the relationships with your advisor and committee members, establishing a foundation for good writing practices will save you time in the long run.

CHAPTER 4

The Write Approach to Crafting Your Dissertation

Unless you're completing a PhD after a previous career as a novelist, the dissertation is probably the longest piece of writing you've ever attempted to write. Even if it's not, it's a difficult genre of writing that isn't quite like anything else. It's important to prepare yourself for not only the elements that need to be included in your dissertation, which the next chapters will address in more detail, but the fact that the actual process of sitting down at your computer and opening a blank document won't always be easy.

The Importance of Playing to Your Strengths

Ellen, a Doctor of Nursing Practice (DNP) student at Walden University, told us that she'd been a procrastinator throughout her academic career. From the last-minute science fair project haphazardly designed from household items to the college term paper completed with the help of energy drinks and all-hours study rooms, she had always produced her best work at the last minute. Early in her dissertation writing process, a colleague recommended that she set a goal to write 300 words a day, to help overcome her tendency to procrastinate. Try as she might, Ellen rarely sat down to write. When she remembered, a bit guiltily, her daily target, and when she *did* make it to her computer, she would usually stare at a blank document for an hour or so before giving up. She progressed well through the literature review process, reading and taking notes on relevant scholarly articles (though her "Chapter 2" document remained empty), and began the process of conducting her qualitative research, but the words still wouldn't come.

The pitfall Ellen was experiencing was a failure to play to her strengths. Though well-meaning, her colleague's advice had the opposite of its intended effect, and Ellen got in her own way by trying to revamp her established mode of working overnight. While for many dissertation writers, setting a target of a certain number of words per day or a certain amount of time spent writing is a great tactic, it didn't help Ellen. She needed the pressure of a deadline to produce content. Her first problem was that it isn't possible to write an entire dissertation during a coffee-fueled all-nighter. Her second problem was that she didn't suddenly become a different type of writer because she was now working on a dissertation. Though habits can and should change, one's tendencies remain the same. Fortunately, what has worked in the past can sometimes be adapted to fit the needs of dissertation writing as well.

In conversation with her dissertation coach, Ellen identified tactics that had worked for her in the past. While she almost always wrote the bulk of her papers the night before they were due, she would usually spend several weeks before the final push researching and outlining her ideas. We brainstormed ways Ellen could "lean in" to this tendency, and she began scheduling "writing marathons" for herself, a few days before the deadlines she and her advisor had agreed upon for the completion of sections of her dissertation. Armed with her annotated bibliography, scribbled ideas, and some caffeine, she produced a twenty-five-page rough draft of her literature review over a weekend of late nights. The pressure of the final push was important to Ellen's writing process and enabled her to produce better work than she could when she attempted to write short sections every day. By determining which sections she was prepared to write (in terms of research conducted and outlines prepared) and setting clear and non-negotiable deadlines for herself, Ellen adapted what had worked for her in the past to the dissertation process.

Think Outside the Box (or the Outline)

Sometimes a student who's inculcated with a linear, traditional academic writing process can find herself suffocated by it. Being open to trying an unusual process can let the writer think productively without conventional restraints.

For her dissertation research, Tasha, a psychology student at University of Virginia, interviewed students who had experienced cognitive dissonance during a university class session. She wanted to know what causes the dissonance and how students resolve it (or don't). She transcribed the forty-five-minute interviews with eight students, who varied widely in the causes and effects of their dissonance experience. Reading the transcripts for qualitative analysis, she found herself mired in indecision about coding and collecting the students' discourse into coherent themes. She studied conventional coding methods, but they weren't working for her.

Tasha's advisor suggested giving up on linear approaches and trying a clustering technique instead. This technique involves starting with a large blank unlined page; Tasha used a big piece of butcher paper. She wrote down two or three potential themes from her interviews, listing quotations that related to each one in another area, adding new potential themes as she thought of them, and drawing arrows between related parts of the cluster. When she thought of something new, she could jot it down in an area close to related words and she could draw arrows to different areas later.

The clustering technique helped free Tasha from prematurely organizing her ideas and then being unsatisfied with them. Though it looked like a big mess, she used it to bring her thoughts into focus and tame them into an outline. Her final dissertation draft was both logical and insightful, and she felt that the clustering exercise was the key to navigating the swamp of data she'd collected. She still uses clustering for starting major writing projects.

Recommended Reading

Ask any professional writer, and they'll tell you that to write well, you need to read a lot. Dissertations or theses are no different. Reading dissertations from recent graduates of your program is a great way to get a feel of what the expectations will be for you. You can also probably reach out to those recent alumni to ask them questions about their process and get insight into the idiosyncrasies of your specific program, without having to use precious office hours from your advisor. Research and academic writing are learned behaviors; very rarely is someone naturally adept at these things. Perhaps the most easily accessible method to picking up these learned behaviors is through books dedicated to writing, research, grammar, and academic work. We've found several academic books that we return to again and again. These books help break down the research and writing process in an easy-to-understand way, while providing new things to think about and new avenues to pursue in my work, along with inspiration during those tough times when we feel like throwing in the towel. Here are some of our favorites.

How to Write a Thesis, by Umberto Eco (translated)

Translated into English for the first time, scholar Umberto Eco's guide to writing a thesis, which he wrote for his own students, provides witty commentary and thoughtful questions about the writing process. Irreverent, smart, and sort of back-to-basics (it was first published in 1977), this book can be especially helpful if you're dealing with information and/or technology overload. Eco describes the thesis-writing process from start to finish, providing guidance for newbies and a wise refresher to those working on any kind of research project.

The Craft of Research (4th Edition), by Wayne C. Booth et al.

This book is a great investment since it's applicable to everyone from undergraduates to graduate students to professionals working on projects in their fields. Written in an accessible manner, the material in this book covers everything involved with research, from beginning research to writing findings and revising the final draft.

The Elements of Style, by William Strunk, Jr. and E. B. White

There are other books that contain the phrase "Elements of Style," but Strunk and White's version has endured for a reason: if you're going to own one book on writing, let it be this one. Don't let the slim volume fool you—this book is packed with valuable writing and composition advice. If you're looking for a bit more pizzazz, consider the early 2000s version with Maira Kalman's beautiful illustrations.

Woe Is I: The Grammarphobe's Guide to Better English in Plain English (3rd Edition), by Patricia T. O'Conner

Grammar can be tricky, but when you're writing a thesis or dissertation, you want to be sure that you're doing everything correctly. This book is a (dare we say it?) fun read on the basics (and not-so-basics) of grammar, with many real-world examples that illustrate O'Conner's points. In this new edition, she gives spelling and punctuation their own chapters, and the bibliography at the end is worth reviewing. It's a great book to have on hand when a grammar question or concern comes up.

They Say/I Say: The Moves That Matter in Academic Writing (3rd Edition), by Gerald Graff and Cathy Birkenstein

This book is helpful in learning how to structure arguments and has a wealth of information about using quotations, summarizing, crafting unique arguments, keeping your voice, and writing in various disciplines and contexts.

How to Write a Lot: A Practical Guide to Productive Academic Writing, by Paul J. Silvia

Academic writing is different from any other kind of writing, as most students know. Whether you're working on your dissertation or thesis, or whether you're up against deadlines for articles for professional advancement, productivity is key. Unfortunately, stress, anxiety, lack of organization, and more can all interfere with successful academic writing—and Silvia knows that. This book is an easy-to-read, down-to-earth guide to working past roadblocks and using specific techniques and tools to increase productivity in your academic writing.

For books about general writing issues, check these out:

Bird by Bird: Some Instructions on Writing and Life, by Anne Lamott

We read chapters of Lamott's classic *Bird by Bird* in my very first class in graduate school. Since then, I've frequently assigned it to my own students. Lamott's book is important for dissertation writers because she acknowledges that writing is hard. Sometimes, you don't feel inspired to write, but you have to persist anyhow and just get the writing done. Through anecdotes about her own life as a writer, and through practical suggestions, Lamott provides writing strategies that can help you get through the tough parts of writing something as ambitious as a dissertation. Lamott advises writers to work through a project "bird by bird"—that is, one small piece at a time. While her advice isn't specifically about dissertations, this tip can make writing a dissertation feel more achievable.

Vernacular Eloquence: What Speech Can Bring to Writing, by Peter Elbow

Elbow is a composition teacher and the author of a number of books about writing. In *Vernacular Eloquence,* he shows how we can use the same sentence structures that we use when we speak in our writing. He's not advocating for a simplistic or colloquial approach, but rather a more natural approach. Elbow argues that by speaking, we learn to use language well, and we can use those same skills in good writing. It's an empowering approach, especially for dissertation writers who may not *think* of themselves as writers, or who may find writing difficult.

Thinking Like Your Editor: How to Write Great Serious Nonfiction and Get It Published, **by Susan Rabiner**

Rabiner's goal in this book is to help authors write nonfiction that gets published, but she has good tips that can apply to dissertation writing, as well. Specifically, her advice to use simple structures to communicate complex ideas is an excellent framework for creating effective scholarly writing. She also discusses how to be persuasive in pitching an idea. This skill can come in handy for dissertation writers in the dissertation proposal stage, when writing abstracts for conference proposals, or when writing grant proposals.

Other Kinds of Graduate School Writing

Conference Abstracts

Attending conferences can be a key piece of your professional development as well as an enjoyable way to meet colleagues and travel. Conferences can take you to cities all over the world, making an incredibly welcome change from the confines of a library study room. Universities and the conferences themselves often offer funding for the travel expenses involved. So, how do you get selected to speak at a conference?

Usually, by submitting an abstract that summarizes the paper you plan to give. These tend to range from 100–500 words, and—like the abstract of your dissertation—include material on the context of the presentation (you'll contextualize the contribution, but it's not a literature review—citations don't tend to have a place in abstracts), your topic/methodology, and what you've determined/its significance. For conference papers, you don't usually need to have completed the paper already, but when you're writing the abstract, speak as if you have (e.g., "this paper shows the significance of . . ." and not "I'm going to investigate the significance of __, and I hope to find that . . ."). Depending on the conference, you may be able to propose not just a paper, but an entire panel consisting of three to five related papers. This is a great way to collaborate with like-minded colleagues and further your professional networking.

Writing a conference paper can be a great complement to your dissertation writing process. If you propose a paper that's related to a section of one of your chapters, you have a time-sensitive reason to draft it. Make sure to give yourself ample time to write the paper. Has Allen ever been guilty of having written a conference paper on the plane to the host city? Maybe, but writing it in the weeks leading up to the trip is always preferable. One of the preeminent scholars in Lauren's field always requested to speak last on his panels, inserted headphones, then wrote notes for the talk he was about to deliver while his colleagues were speaking, but that is definitely not polite or advisable.

Remember as you write a conference paper that reading aloud takes much longer than silent reading, so it's important to practice and time your work. A good rule of thumb is that one typed page (double spaced, twelve pt. Times New Roman font) takes at least two minutes to read, so ten pages is the absolute longest paper you'd want to deliver in a twenty-minute presentation, and making it a little shorter would give you time to slow down and deliver it more engagingly. So, if you find yourself trying to finish your essay while flying the friendly skies, you can just aim for eight pages. As a bonus to not pushing your length to the max, everyone in the room will be grateful that you've left more time for the Q&A session.

When delivering a conference paper, general rules of good public speaking apply. The more you can speak directly to and make eye contact with your audience rather than staring down at your notes and reading each word, the more engaging the presentation will be. Be careful to stay within the time allowed and follow any rules for visual aids, etc., given by the conference organizers. Panel discussions also include a time for Q&A. This can be a great forum for interesting discussion, but there are a couple of common issues to watch out for. Some audience members treat the "asking of a question" as an opportunity to speak at length about their own research, which can be addressed with a reply along the lines of "that's really interesting, and is related (cough, very loosely) to the point I made about __." Some individuals will be argumentative for the sake of it or ask if you've thought about a single obscure point or read a single obscure article that is usually key to the individual's own research or agenda. To those commentators, a graceful "thank you for pointing that out. I'll be sure to think about/research it" is well-placed. In general, though, such sessions can be a great way to develop new ideas for your dissertation or your future academic work.

It's important to give yourself time to make connections and network with colleagues in your field. Don't blow off the cocktail hours, receptions, etc. You might miss out on free food and drink, for one thing, but more importantly, these are the ideal venues during which to connect with individuals you wouldn't otherwise have encountered. You may be a social butterfly and have no problems in such events, but if you find yourself feeling awkward around a room full of new faces, try showing interest in the people you meet and asking them questions about their studies and their work. You will likely find that when you show interest in others, they will return the favor!

Grant Proposals

Depending on your research and your research needs, sometimes you need additional funding through grants. Some universities have internal grants. For example, Lauren's program guaranteed funding for the first three years of the degree, but fourth-year funding was competitive and awarded based on a proposal for a funding grant. Some universities offer summer funding, which enables you to complete important supplementary activities like conducting archival research or attending conferences. You may also be able to obtain external funding, sponsored by different professional bodies in your field, nonprofits, or governmental organizations. Whether you're in graduate school or working in your field, knowing how to write an effective grant proposal is beneficial for obtaining additional funding for your project or team. If you're a professor, securing grants can be crucial to your ongoing work and research. Once you're lucky enough to have a grant proposal accepted, you then have to submit progress reports and final reports to the funding agencies. Importantly, you can't win a grant if you don't apply for one. Just going through the process of applying puts you ahead of all the others who were too scared to go for it. If your proposal is not accepted, you can revise and resubmit during the next grant cycle using the time in between to develop your proposal further and strengthen your case. There's really nothing to lose by applying.

Each grant process is a little different, based on your discipline and research intentions, but there are some general guidelines to keep in mind. Learning some general grant-writing tips can help make the process less stressful.

Here are some basic things to keep in mind for grant proposals:

- Start early. It never fails; the less time you have for a grant proposal, the more things will be thrown at you or go wrong, or the more demands on your time will suddenly appear. Starting early is never a bad thing, no matter what the project—but especially grant proposals.
- Read the directions. It sounds simple, but lots of people don't read and follow the directions. Address everything they ask, and preemptively answer questions that aren't asked.

Before you start writing a grant proposal, it's usually best to have some questions answered, on paper or in your own mind, as these can help guide your writing and give you some clarity about direction and focus.

- Is this a pilot study?
- Is this for dissertation research? Experimental? Fieldwork? Postdoc. work? Are you looking for a stipend to buy you some time to write a book, or are you seeking funding for a pretty big, multiyear study?

- What is the topic, and why is it important?
- What are your research questions, and why do they matter?
- What methodology are you using, and what kind of research are you doing?

Not only are these important questions to keep in mind before you start your proposal, but they can even help shape your funding searches.

Think about your audience. Who will be reading your proposal? Does your proposal align with the organization's mission and goals? Are these readers familiar with the kind of research you're doing or not? How much background and explanation do you need to provide? What kind of material will be most persuasive to the selection committee? Most reviewers want to know what your goals and outcomes are, why your research/project is significant, and what your criteria for success are.

Make sure you follow the submission guidelines. This cannot be overstated. Follow the guidelines exactly as stated; you aren't exempt, even if you write a note explaining why you haven't followed the directions. Nothing will discredit you faster than not following directions. Follow the headings provided, make sure all sections are labeled appropriately and include everything the guidelines require.

Outline your plan clearly, professionally, and logically. Your writing will provide the grant committee with a sense of who you are as a person and researcher, and it will convey your grasp of the material and general knowledge of your topic. Being thorough and intentional with your writing will enhance your professionalism. Grant proposals aren't the place to write expansively; they favor concise and direct writing.

Before you submit your grant proposal, it's always a good idea to ask people who are established in your field to review it. You might want a statistician to review your methodology, for example. If your grant proposal is rejected, don't give up! Take any feedback to heart and get to work on revising and strengthening the proposal to get it ready for the next funding cycle. Talk to others in your field or a trusted mentor to see where you can improve, and what to keep in mind for the next time you submit. Finally, don't forget to add grants that you've written to your CV. You can include unawarded grants too. Future employers will take notice of your ability to write grants and, knowing that it takes practice to learn the skill and that many grant proposals are rejected, will likely be inclined to give you a shot at writing grants for them.

Resumes and Curriculum Vitae

Applying for a new job can be stressful, and often, the key to getting your foot in the door for a second look or an interview is a well-organized, thoughtful resume or CV. A good resume or CV will provide a snapshot of your experience, education, and professional interests, but it can be intimidating to organize and present everything in a formatted document.

What's the difference between a resume and a CV? There are usually a few main differences: the purpose, length, and formatting. A CV, or curriculum vitae, is typically at least two pages long and spans a long period of time. It details educational history, awards received, research publications, and so forth. It has a lot of details about each entry and doesn't change based on the job to which you're applying.

On the other hand, a resume is a much more concise document and should be two pages *at most* and is generally only one page. It should be adapted to fit best the position to which you're applying, and you usually have a lot more flexibility in how this is formatted and what material is covered. While you don't need to rewrite the whole document for each position, you can reorganize it to highlight different information. You'll also want to use words from the job description in order to get past the algorithms designed to weed out applicants.

For the most part, in the United States, a CV is usually used when applying for a job in academia or research, and a resume is used in other situations.

Dos and Don'ts

Do include all pertinent information, especially current contact information.

Don't cover every inch of the page with information. Leave enough white space to make it easily readable. Use a simple font and minimal embellishment. For a resume, make sure it's tailored to the specific position to which you're applying.

Do read it multiple times for spelling, grammar, and punctuation. A professional editor can provide an objective eye and critical feedback, as well as talk with you about what you'd like to convey to a potential employer.

Don't just focus on submitting the resume or CV as fast as possible after hearing about the job. This is the first impression the selection committee will have of you; make it a good one.

<u>Do</u> highlight your achievements and accomplishments, include soft skills (e.g., communication competencies), and include membership in professional organizations.

<u>Don't</u> embellish your experience, awards, or employment. Be honest with your resume or CV. If you've misrepresented yourself, chances are, this will come back to haunt you, and could even result in termination from employment.

<u>Do</u> use active voice.

<u>Don't</u> use passive voice.

<u>Do</u> model your CV after your professors (copies of which are likely on their faculty web pages).

<u>Don't</u> try to get too fancy with your layout and/or font selection. Keep it simple.

Consider sending your resume or CV to a professional editing service to polish it up and ensure proper formatting. A professional, objective outsider can provide you with fresh eyes and expert advice on how to make it the best it can be. It's more than a truism that you have to spend money to make money. If you put in the effort and the resources to make a professional CV, then you will be taken more seriously by prospective employers.

Finally, and perhaps the most important "do" on this list, is to articulate to your prospective employer how valuable the experience of having completed a dissertation is. You may have learned to research and apply for grants, secure funding for your work; you cultivated professional time management skills, balancing the dissertation writing process with the rest of your work and life; you developed impeccable research skills, sifting through endless articles and books and synthesizing their ideas into a summary of the state of a whole field; you conducted original research on your subject, and/or developed new ideas on it. You contributed to human knowledge. While many of these things are taken for granted among the academic community, they are laudable skills, so it's worth spending time curating the verbiage you'll use to describe them on your resume and in your cover letter, and selecting the anecdotes that provide the best evidence of your professionalism for use in an interview setting.

Cover Letters

Cover letters are a great place to explain in detail skills and experiences (like having written a dissertation!) that make you a great fit for a particular role, but which may require more space than the resume format allows. There are two keys to a great cover letter. First, it has to show what separates you from other candidates who may have similar qualifications. Second, it should confirm for your prospective employer that you'll not only be able to perform the function of the role, but will also fit into the organizational culture and that your values align with those of the company. To accomplish this, a good cover letter must be carefully tailored to the job in question. While you can probably use the same resume, or close to it, for multiple job applications (maybe with tweaks to what you emphasize and your professional summary), a cover letter really needs to be specific to the job listing. Few things make a hiring manager lose interest in a candidate's application faster than realizing their cover letter was written in response to a different role. If it's worth applying for the job, it's worth rewriting your cover letter to be considered for it.

Plagiarism

Plagiarism is a serious problem in academia, even at the graduate-school level, and new tools like the GPT-3 chatbot are only making the problem worse. But humans are much greater offenders than AI for dissertation plagiarism. If you Google "write my dissertation," you'll find fields of dissertation writing mills. We sometimes have prospective clients who email Dissertation Editor and ask us to write their dissertations for them. We reply to them and explain that that would be plagiarism and could potentially cause them to be kicked out of school.

So, what *is* plagiarism? Thankfully, academic plagiarism has definite parameters. While each university (and often each doctoral program) has its own code of academic conduct, most of them share a basic definition of plagiarism. In short, plagiarism is committed when you present someone else's idea as your own or fail to properly cite information from preexisting sources. There are three basic forms of plagiarism: 1.) Using the exact wording from an existing source (e.g., book, article, newspaper, or class lecture) without using quotation marks to identify the quoted content and citing its source; 2.) Describing or appropriating concepts or information learned from another source without citing it; and 3.) Having someone else write your paper for you. Simply put, if you include words or ideas that aren't yours and present them as if they were, that is plagiarism.

Leroy, a psychology student at Capella university, sent us a lengthy dissertation on marriage and trauma in Haitian culture. Much of his project came from his experience as a marriage counselor working to help Haitian couples reject a Haitian outlook that expected the trauma of a broken cultural history to assert itself in their relationships. But to provide a background of critical perspectives that helped contextualize Haitian trauma, Leroy had, in no uncertain terms, ransacked Encyclopedia Britannica. An editor met with Leroy and listened to him talk about the stress of working on the dissertation for the past seven years while teaching adjunct classes at two colleges. He was desperate to finish the project and without a plan or the wherewithal for developing his ideas, he had tried recycling the encyclopedia. His editor helped Leroy steer away from plagiarism by asking him questions about what was central to his study. He came away from that meeting with a refocused understanding of what his project was. Leroy and his editor listed out his main ideas and pinpointed what he should develop.

Plagiarism can be as short as four words in a row or as long and vague as your dissertation's entire premise. Whether intentional or inadvertent, it is critically important to be careful by avoiding plagiarism throughout the dissertation writing process. Aside from being dishonest, one of the main problems with academic plagiarism is that it undermines the scholarly process. Plagiarism steals from the hard work of previous scholars without giving credit where it is due. And it steals from your readers' perceptions of you and your contribution to the field. Your dissertation is meant to be an original piece of scholarship that offers new insights into your field of study. While your dissertation will be supported and corroborated by a wealth of previous literature, it must be clear exactly how *your* original ideas are situated within the scholarship of your field.

Whether intentional or not, plagiarism's risks far outweigh any possible benefit. Unintentional plagiarism may just bring a stiff reprimand from your doctoral advisor and an order that you rewrite the offending passages. However, if the plagiarism is proven to be intentional, then you may be expelled from your university and barred from realizing your dream of earning your PhD. Your PhD experience will be done, but in the worst way.

But the temptation to plagiarize comes easily with the constant availability of an endless stream of information available through the Internet. Copying and pasting information from a book or a website into your working document takes only a few seconds, but the Information Age has also made it easier for inquiring minds to catch those who have played fast and loose with their sources. Websites like Turnitin, iThenticate, and Plagium make it very easy for your advisor to tell if your content is the least bit unoriginal. Most universities have institutional accounts for plagiarism-checking software and will submit your dissertation for analysis before accepting it. Not only will these sites show what content has been plagiarized, they will also reveal the source from which the content was derived. More simply, one can just copy questionable phrases from your paper and put them into Google to see if there is potential plagiarism.

Plagiarism-checking software tends to return the amount of text that matches other sources as a percentage, and different institutions may have different requirements (e.g., under 10 percent, under 20 percent). Remember that your target isn't and can't be 0 percent, (because presumably you've quoted from existing texts, referenced articles that have also been referenced in other published scholarship, and used common expressions or phrases in your writing—and the plagiarism detector will flag citations too, so it really is impossible to achieve a 0 percent on a plagiarism report), but the bigger the number, the more likely a plagiarism issue is present.

Plagiarism is a danger, even if you don't mean to do it. Lazy practices such as not using quotation marks around unique phrases can leave you vulnerable to what can best be termed "accidental plagiarism." The verdict is still out on whether the late historian Stephen Ambrose intentionally used identical phrases from another historian (Kirkpatrick, 2002a).

Ambrose apologized publicly, though he argued that he was merely guilty of sloppy research practices rather than academic dishonesty. His reputation was forever tarnished as a result (Kirkpatrick, 2002a). Don't let something similar happen to your dissertation after years of grueling doctoral research! Be careful to cite ALL your sources. Make sure also to investigate your advisor's and institution's expectations and definitions surrounding self-plagiarism. Often, work that even you yourself have previously completed and submitted for academic credit or published (i.e., a relevant term paper for a graduate seminar) is also off limits, as it's not original to your dissertation. Although, you can and should *quote* your previously published work.

To avoid plagiarism, quotation marks and parentheses may be your most important allies. Use them religiously during the draft phases of the dissertation writing process. Never assume that you'll remember to go back and add a citation at a later point in the process; enough time might pass that you forget where you found the information or even that it was a quotation. Even if you've only used three or four words strung together that you liked from another source, quote and cite them. In academia, especially in the humanities, it's difficult to over-cite your sources. Those reading your work prefer to see the footprint of where you have been intellectually (i.e., what you have read and how you came to your conclusions). When in doubt, err on the side of caution and cite your source. Remember that it is much easier, and will save you time in the long run, to cite your sources correctly when you first identify them during the research process. If you assume you'll remember where you read the information or leave yourself a note saying, "find this citation later," it's likely to take double the time, and your future self won't thank you for it!

That said, while you should always cite your sources, your dissertation committee does not want to read a dissertation full of quotations. Overusing quotations implies to the reader that you don't have anything original to say. You should paraphrase (i.e., completely rewrite) and synthesize quotations into your own thoughts and words as much as possible, especially with secondary sources. Just don't forget that paraphrased material still requires a source citation, including the page number or page range. While directly quoting primary sources can be necessary for some disciplines (history and religious studies in particular), the dissertation should generally be replete with your own thoughts and insights about primary source content and previous scholarship. Avoid direct quotations whenever possible and certainly never begin or end your paragraphs with them.

Another helpful tool to avoid plagiarism is citation and research management software like Endnote, RefWorks, or the open-source Firefox extension, Zotero. These programs can help you organize your sources and centralize your research in one place. You can also download important articles and texts to keep them readily available for later use. This way, if you wonder whether a certain phrase is yours or someone else's, you can do a quick online search to be sure. There are pros and cons to using citation and referencing software, which will be discussed in greater detail in the section titled "Citation Software Systems: Pros, Cons, and an Overview of Options."

The simplest advice is *don't plagiarize*! It might seem like a little sloppy source work increases the efficiency of the dissertation process, but aside from being intellectually deceitful and putting you in danger of expulsion, it is also counterproductive to your long-term career viability. Pulitzer Prize–winning historian Doris Kearns Goodwin had to resign from the Pulitzer committee and from the PBS MacNeil-Lehrer *News Hour* after it came to light that she had used significant portions of another book in her 1987 work on the Kennedy family (Kirkpatrick, 2002b). She is not the first prominent scholar to lose credibility, and by no means will she be the last. Luckily, with some careful effort, plagiarism is easy to avoid, and you can turn in your dissertation confident that it is completely original writing.

When to Start From Scratch

Joe, who was working on his doctorate in communication at CU Boulder, came to us for editing of his literature review chapter on interpersonal communication theory, a sixty-page behemoth with hundreds of sources included. His editor was about fifteen pages into the chapter when the drastic shifts in his writing style started to feel fishy. She copied a passage of text into Google and found that some sections of the chapter were lifted from a 2007 dissertation on almost exactly the same topic. We let Joe know that we'd have to stop editing until he addressed the plagiarism issue. Joe had come across the dissertation early in his research, and it contained exactly the same seminal research on his topic he needed to cite, so he added most of its sources—and some of its text—directly into his annotated bibliography. The other author's words made their way into his chapter, and a huge plagiarism issue arose.

Joe wanted to fix the problem, so he set to work revising the chapter. He came back to us for editing again, telling us the plagiarism was all fixed. The editor set to work on the chapter, but soon found that the problem remained. Joe had done a great deal of work on paraphrasing, so none of the 2007 dissertation's exact words remained, but Joe was still plagiarizing. He still cited the same studies as the 2007 dissertation *and* synthesized their significance in the same way. Even though nothing had been copied and pasted into this revised version, Joe was still using someone else's ideas and work.

Eventually, Joe found that if he wanted to complete his literature review the right way, he'd have to start over. The other author's views on the subject were too ingrained in this version, so he went back to the drawing board—reading key articles again and interpreting them from his own perspective. Eventually, a stronger chapter with a different argument emerged, and Joe submitted original work to his advisor. Sometimes, whether it's a whole chapter or a shorter section, it's worth considering whether it's necessary to start over, rather than revise existing work. This applies not only to plagiarism but sometimes also to major revisions. If a chapter section requires major organizational and content changes, make sure to pause and think about whether revising the text that's already there is the most efficient way to move forward. Sometimes it will be, but there are cases where gritting your teeth and starting with a clean slate will actually save you time and make your life easier. Remember that whether or not you use any of the same words from the first draft in the finished dissertation, the ideas and research behind them are still there, and the previous drafts were anything but wasted effort.

Writer's Block

We're tempted to say something controversial here. In fact, we will: writer's block doesn't really exist, at least not in the context of a dissertation. Is it sometimes impossible to find words that feel aligned with the importance of the ideas you have? Absolutely. Will you spend more time than you care to admit staring at a blank document or piece of paper during your writing career? Yes, you will. Does the whole thing sometimes feel insurmountable? It definitely does.

However, it's easy to give the term "writer's block" too much power, and at times even use it as an excuse: "I would have finished my literature review chapter, but I had writer's block." A useful shift in mindset entails having realistic, flexible goals for completing different types of writing work and writing preparation work. It also includes thinking strategically about when you're most likely to accomplish different pieces of that writing work. If you sit down at your computer with the sole goal of creating a brilliant concluding sentence for your dissertation that includes a witty pun and encapsulates the core of your ideas, you may not be able to do that. If you sit down to achieve a piece of work to advance your progress toward completing your conclusion, you're much more likely to walk away from your desk having written something. You may discover that, by forcing yourself to write, you discover thoughts that you didn't know you had. Or, perhaps, it's that you didn't have those thoughts until you gave yourself the time to have them. More than any other cause, writers can block themselves by not writing. Don't be your own block!

Give Yourself Permission to Pivot

As discussed earlier in this chapter, different writers work differently, and it's important to play to your strengths. However, even if you're the most linear and organized of writers, a dissertation cannot be written one word at a time in a row. If you get stuck on the paragraph you're working on, give yourself permission to shift your attention to a section that comes more easily. Really don't feel like trying to write is the best use of your time right now? Better to acknowledge that and shift your attention elsewhere. Is there an article you need to read and make notes on? Been meaning to clean up your reference list? Those tasks might be a better use of your time.

Use Your Most Productive Time Well

It's important to know yourself and to identify when your brain is most likely to be capable of its most critical thinking. Think about when you do your best work. Early in the morning? Late at night? In a particular workspace, or when your desk is set up in a certain way? Identify your optimal time and situation, and make sure to use that to sit down to accomplish the trickiest pieces of dissertation writing.

Though many writers like using various websites as writing tools, if you find that the Internet is a distraction, you may want to turn off your Wi-Fi, and it may be best to silence your phone and put it in a drawer during your assigned writing time. On one occasion when Lauren was trying to research for an undergraduate term paper, she turned to her roommate to complain about how easy it is to get distracted, quickly toggling from the browser window containing research to the one containing social media accounts. "Why don't you try using self-control?" Lauren's roommate asked. "I'm trying," Lauren opined back, offended, before her roommate told her that self-control was the name of a free app that blocks your access to certain websites for a set duration, while allowing you to use the Internet for other research. Self-control, both in the real sense and the virtual one, can help you create a space to work on your writing for an extended period of time. On the other hand, don't forget to give your eyes and wrists a break. Look out of a window for half a minute now and then. Get up and stretch. Consider taking a short walk to think about your idea. Or better yet, don't think about your idea for a little bit. Let your mind run things over in the background. Do a chore. Run an errand. Something as simple as brushing your teeth may work wonders.

Find Strategies to Get Unstuck

Ben, who was writing a philosophy dissertation at the University of Washington, had a habit of spending hours staring at the same sentence in his dissertation, unable to move on until he felt that the words and flow were exactly right. Try as he might, whatever strategies he implemented, he had a hard time shifting his attention to other aspects of the dissertation or even doing other dissertation work until he felt that the words he was writing at the time were perfect. To get out of his own way, he had to get away from the computer. He took to recording himself speaking using his cell phone while he took long, meandering drives through the rainy streets of Seattle. When he got home, he'd transcribe what he'd recorded, and was suddenly able to organize and refine his thoughts once he had a first draft on paper.

Now that you have selected your topic, taken a realistic look at the work-life balance challenges that might emerge, put together your team of experts to guide you through the process, prepared yourself for possible challenges that might emerge when dealing with those experts, and established a foundation for good writing practices, it's time to start your dissertation. In the chapters that follow, we will walk you through the nuts and bolts of dissertation preparation from conducting background research to acing your defense. It's a long journey with many steps along the way! However, with our road map, you'll at least have a sense of where you're headed and not feel like each new chapter is uncharted territory.

CHAPTER 5

Off the Starting Blocks: How to Begin Your Dissertation

There are several milestones to reach during the dissertation writing process. Rest assured as you meet these milestones, step-by-step, you are getting closer to achieving your goal: getting your dissertation approved by the university. One of the first milestones is to have your topic approved by your advisor. If your study dissertation process includes conducting research, once you have agreed on a research topic, you will want to create a research proposal to send for ethical approval that includes the background of your topic, your research questions, hypotheses, and detailed information on your methodology. You will likely submit your proposal for ethical approval to your university's institutional review board (IRB). In some cases, if you are working with participants from certain organizations, they may have their own ethics committee that would need to approve your proposal as well. Once you have obtained ethical approval, you can begin the data collection process. Often, collecting data is time consuming and, therefore, this is a good time to start writing your literature review and methodology chapters and send them to your advisor to review and provide feedback.

After your data have been collected and your hypotheses tested, you can begin to write up your results and discussion chapters, which you should also send to your advisor to review and provide feedback as you go. Once your advisor has approved all your chapters, it's time to send the entire dissertation draft to your committee to review and provide feedback. When your committee has agreed that your draft is ready, you can submit your final draft for approval by the Dean if required (again, this process depends on your university, so be sure to consult your graduate student handbook regularly to make sure you're taking all required steps).

This chapter addresses the first several elements and chapters you'll need to work toward to lay the foundation for your dissertation. First, it addresses various strategies for organizing the dissertation, before moving to a discussion of what should be included in your abstract and introduction. It concludes with an extended discussion of the literature review chapter and the process of identifying and vetting sources to include.

Dissertation Organization

If you are unclear what your dissertation should include, there is a basic five-chapter formula you can follow outlined in the next section. While this formula is often followed by PhD students, others may find their dissertations require additional chapters or a different layout completely. If you are unsure of which structure you want to follow for your particular project, the five-chapter formula is a great place to start.

The Five-Chapter Formula

Writing a dissertation is a significant undertaking, but the good thing is that you're not reinventing the wheel. Most dissertations follow a standard five-chapter formula. In some disciplines, like the fine arts and some social sciences like economics, dissertations can take different forms or have different components. However, most disciplines follow the five-chapter model. Even within the five-chapter rubric, different areas of study may have some variation in each chapter. Your graduate program will provide you with specific guidelines that your school and program require.

The basic chapter headings of a dissertation generally include:

- Chapter 1: Introduction
- Chapter 2: Literature Review
- Chapter 3: Methodology
- Chapter 4: Results
- Chapter 5: Discussion and Conclusion

These might look very different based on whether you're doing a qualitative versus quantitative dissertation, but these are the general chapter themes that typically compose a dissertation.

While most dissertations follow the standard five-chapter outline, there are always exceptions. Find out what your program requires and if there are any variations on this method of organization. Become familiar with what your specific program wants and proceed accordingly. In what follows, I'll provide tips and suggestions for how to tackle each of these chapters, so that you can prepare yourself for the writing process when you reach that stage of your dissertation.

Other Organizational Options

While most dissertations follow the five-chapter formula, some fields or departments offer different choices or more flexibility. In the humanities, for instance, the organizational structure may be entirely up to the dissertation writer. There may not even be a specific requirement for the number of chapters required. If this is the case, be sure to work closely with your advisor to ensure that your expectations are the same. For instance, Aaron, who was studying anthropology at the University of British Columbia, dealt with an unexpected challenge near the end of his writing process, when he realized that he had a five-chapter dissertation planned, but his advisor was expecting him to write six chapters, including one solely devoted to his theoretical framework. Fortunately, he was able to make the case that it made more sense to expand the length of his existing chapters with additional theory rather than add an entirely new one, but the outcome could have been much more disastrous. If you are permitted flexibility, extra caution and communication during the planning and outlining process can save you a great deal of headache.

If you are allowed to determine your own organizational structure, be sure to spend an ample amount of time thinking about how it makes the most sense to you to break down your ideas, as well as what will make the most sense for your reader.

A few options are thematic, chronological, and compartmentalized. Take, for example, a literature dissertation on the work of Leo Tolstoy. A thematic approach might deal with different aspects of the texts in different chapters (Chapter 1: War in Tolstoy's Work; Chapter 2: Peace in Tolstoy's Work; Chapter 3: Tolstoy's Use of Natural vs Mechanical Imagery). A chronological option might break the structure down into time periods (Chapter 1: Tolstoy's Early Work; Chapter 2: Middle Period; Chapter 3: Tolstoy's Late Work). A compartmentalized approach might address one text in each chapter (Chapter 1: *The Death of Ivan Ilyich*; Chapter 2: *Anna Karenina*; Chapter 3: *War and Peace*). In any of these examples, our budding Tolstoy expert's dissertation is *much* too broad, and they should return to the section on selecting a topic, but the principles and options remain the same.

More recently, some institutions have allowed writers to produce dissertations composed of three self-contained articles. A great way to move from dissertation to publication, writers of this type of dissertation write each of the chapters (usually three of them, plus an introduction and conclusion) as if it is an article for publication in a certain target journal. This means that there is likely some amount of repetition (the literature review of each article might be similar, for example), which is an important question to raise with your advisor. If this type of dissertation is an option, be sure to pay close attention to the requirements of your target journals and the types of pieces they publish during the planning process. Done right, this type of dissertation can lead very quickly and seamlessly into an emerging scholar's first (or first of several) publication.

Writing Your Abstract

What Is an Abstract?

An abstract is a succinct piece of writing that tells potential readers what a paper, book, dissertation, or other text is about. Abstracts are short and highly informative. For most APA projects, they tend to be between 150 and 250 words long (American Psychological Association, 2020). They should entice readers, make them interested in your work, and help them determine if they want to read your paper, dissertation, or project in its entirety. Although the abstract is located at the beginning of the dissertation and is one of the first aspects of your dissertation that the reader will see, it isn't the first piece of writing you should start with—in fact, it's often the last, as it is essentially a summary of your project.

When Do Dissertation Writers Use Abstracts?

You may be required to submit an abstract of your dissertation as part of your dissertation proposal. In addition, dissertation writers are often required to include an abstract of their dissertation when they submit the final version to their dissertation committee, dissertation advisor, or institution. As discussed in the previous chapter, if you decide to present a paper or a part of your dissertation at an academic conference, you will likely need to submit an abstract as part of the application process. Similarly, if you decide to publish a chapter of your dissertation in a book or in a journal, you will likely need to submit an abstract to the editor. Applications for grants and fellowships also frequently call for abstracts of your dissertation or research. Even though abstracts are short (journals, conferences, and academic departments have different length requirements), they need to pack a punch. The abstract should be a concise description of the work and should make sense by itself, even to someone who hasn't read the full dissertation.

Points Your Abstract Should Address

Your abstract should include several points. Be sure to include the following with your abstract:

- What problem are you addressing?
- Why should the reader care about your research problem and the results? There are thousands of research papers available; why should yours be the one they want to read?
- What methods did you use to solve this problem?
- What were your results?
- What are the implications of your findings in your field and in general? Can your results be generalized to wider populations?

Precise Language

Writing an abstract can be difficult. Your job is to communicate lots of information using a limited number of words. You only have a few sentences to devote to the elements outlined above. This requires precise, effective, and evocative use of language. Choose each word carefully to convey your intended meaning. Active voice is preferable to passive voice in abstracts, just as it is in effective academic writing more generally.

Considerations

When writing your abstract, keep in mind the keywords that people will search for when looking for your paper. Include these important keywords in your abstract so your work will appear in their search results. Each journal, conference, or academic program may have different specifications for an abstract. So, make sure you're familiar with the specific submission guidelines for your project. In carpentry, the saying "measure twice, cut once" is a watchword, given that once the board is cut, it can't be uncut. While you can "uncut" the changes you make to your article, it can be time-consuming and frustrating to do so. That's why it's always better to map out exactly what is required before starting.

Writing Your Introduction

When you work on your dissertation, you submit chapters to your advisor, your chair, and perhaps an editor. You might even have a dissertation critique group and share chapters with each other. Many students write the introduction first as they begin their process, knowing that they will have to edit it dramatically after completing all the other chapters. Once you've written the entire dissertation, you have a better idea of the goals of your paper and the aim of your study. With the other chapters completed, you will know how to introduce those chapters without repeating yourself. The trick of writing an introduction is to craft this information in such a way that it will hook the reader, orient them to your project, and give them a road map of what to expect throughout the dissertation. One of the pitfalls of writing an introduction is inadvertently repeating yourself. In good-quality writing, the same sentence should not appear more than once in the document. Avoid the urge to copy and paste to or from your other chapters. Even though you are supposed to keep your thesis and your main claims visible to your reader, you have to develop those claims simultaneously.

You will want to repeat keywords and consider your ideas in different ways, but copying and pasting—even when you are copying and pasting your own writing—is never the right move.

Goals of the Introduction

The introduction should inform the reader about the background of the topic, the gap in the literature, and how you are going to fill that gap. It should also emphasize why your research is unique, what you are adding to the conversation about this topic, and where your work fits in within a larger context. Most importantly, why should the reader care about what you have to say? What were your findings? What are the implications of those findings? You want to prepare the reader for the rest of your dissertation. Think of it like this: give the reader an overall idea of your paper, then give them the specifics. Reading other completed dissertations, scholarly textbooks, and/or journal articles to see how those writers handle the introduction can be very helpful.

Points to Remember

The introduction should give the reader an overall preview and outline of the paper; however, it also needs to have some specific, practical goals. You need to explain your methodology. Why did you choose the tools you used for your research? How did you use them? What influenced your decisions? You also need to define your key terms. Yes, your readers will most likely be in your field and many laypeople may also know your key terms, but different people may come to different understandings of a term, and you need to define how you are using it in your dissertation.

Writing the Literature Review

The first phase of writing a dissertation is conducting a detailed review of literature in your field to determine which topics researchers have already addressed and which they have not. Before we delve into the intricacies of the literature review process, it's worth noting that it can be one of the most labor-intensive parts of the dissertation process. It involves a significant amount of reading, and many dissertation writers underestimate the time they will spend searching for articles, reviewing abstracts to determine if they are relevant, taking notes on the important aspects of those sources, organizing those notes, synthesizing them into a thematically organized framework, and writing the literature review chapter itself.

Helen, a busy professional who was completing her psychology dissertation through National University, had difficulty finding time to work on her dissertation and was stranded in her literature review. She was not sure of her research question, so the choice of what to include remained unclear. Then, in a History of Psychology class, she was asked to complete an in-class writing assignment about a personal experience with Kurt Lewin's three stages of change (unfreezing, change, refreezing). This is what Helen wrote:

> "Two years ago, I decided to train for my first marathon. Although I was already a moderate runner at the time, I knew that training for a marathon would involve a drastic change to my daily schedule and sleep and eating habits. Looking back on the experience, I can see how Kurt Lewin's three-step process of change occurred during my training months.

The unfreezing stage began when I made the initial decision to begin training. I started reading about the process online and decided to follow a four-month-long, structured training schedule. I began preparations by purchasing a new pair of running shoes, ordering supplies like a water bottle belt and energy gels for my long runs, looking up carb and protein-heavy meals, and setting a start date for my training runs to begin.

During the change stage, I implemented the training schedule and alterations to my daily routine. Prior to this process, I would often run in the evenings. After starting training, I had to restructure my days so that I could run early in the morning, which meant that I had to sleep earlier in the evening. I also implemented new stretches and set aside two mornings each week for cross-training exercises. Transitioning my sleep and wake cycle was difficult to adjust to, but gradually this became easier. I also had to start refusing late-night activities with friends if I had an early morning long run scheduled the next day.

I adjusted to my new routine as I entered the freezing stage. I experienced greater stability and found it easier to follow the morning training schedule. Even after completing the marathon, I have maintained the routine of running in the morning instead of the evening. I also periodically go for long runs on the weekend and implement the same meals and sleep routine that I used during my training months. I ran my second marathon this past January and found the training process to be much easier to transition into since I have incorporated many of the training behaviors into my daily routine."

When Helen got her writing back, she found that her professor had praised it and had written, "I wish all dissertation writers would realize that they have to give something up, like you did for marathoning!" This comment smacked Helen in the face. Even though the professor didn't know her dissertation dilemma, the remark spurred a new direction for Helen's progress. She realized that if she could make such big changes in her life to run a marathon, she could also do so to write her dissertation. Why in the world did she think she didn't have to revamp her lifestyle to complete such an important project? Once Helen started to plan her dissertation work in stages analogous to her marathon training, giving up some beloved activities and adding goal-directed actions, her dissertation took form, and she completed her defense a semester earlier than expected. Now, whenever she takes on a major endeavor, she asks herself, "What am I going to give up? What do I need to freeze? What new mindset do I need?"

While the literature review process might be something of a marathon, this process of research can help you find novel approaches to old questions or help you discover ways to apply tried and true methods to new and understudied situations. In the modern era, information is easily accessible via the Internet. There's no shortage of conversations happening online about every possible subject; however, not all this information is reliable or suitable for use in scholarly writing. It's important to distinguish "scholarly sources" from the rest and only rely on those scholarly sources when conducting research.

A scholarly source is another term for a peer-reviewed source, which means that the book or article has gone through a process of peer review to ensure that its methods and findings are sound, well-argued, and worthy of publication. The term "peer review" is critical because it is this process of scholarly vetting that ensures only rigorous and well-researched material is published. Not all scholarly sources are research studies. Some examples of scholarly sources include articles from academic journals, published theses or dissertations, conference proceedings, handbooks, and monographs. But you have to look closely at any source. Some so-called academic journals are predatory journals that will publish anything so long as the writer pays for publication. And some so-called monographs are self-published and did not receive a traditional peer review. Remember, the key distinction between vetted sources and non-vetted sources is whether the publication has gone through a peer-review process.

So, what types of sources are *not* scholarly sources? Things like newspaper or magazine articles, book reviews, advocacy or opinion-based articles and essays, and pretty much any sources that don't contain references are not peer-reviewed or scholarly texts. Articles about scholarly topics written by journalists may still be factually correct and worthwhile but are not considered scholarly sources. While these have their place in certain kinds of papers and writing, they're typically not appropriate for a thesis or dissertation. Most websites are not scholarly sources, including encyclopedia pages, Healthline, and Wikipedia. These should never be used for a thesis or dissertation: *especially* Wikipedia, as with a wiki, anyone can update or alter the content. Therefore, it is *never* a credible academic source, even if much of the content may be correct. Likewise, websites like the Centers for Disease Control and Prevention (CDC) are credible, but not necessarily scholarly.

Trade publications can be tricky. These are often magazines or journals in a specific industry or field. Examples include

Library Journal, Attorney at Law Magazine, and *Psychology Today.* While they might seem like scholarly sources because of their specialized nature, they're popular sources for the general public and aren't appropriate to use for your research project. That said, they still have value. They can be a great place to start your background reading on your topic and can work as a general information hub to point you toward scholarly sources or trends to explore further in academic journal articles. In other words, feel free to use non-scholarly sources for your own personal exploration of a topic, but when it comes time to start writing, restrict your citations to scholarly sources only and make sure that you can back up your claims with information gathered from scholarly sources.

So where do you find scholarly sources? University libraries usually have a reference desk, and research librarians can be invaluable resources for any questions you have during your dissertation research process. Online, scholarly sources are typically found in databases like JSTOR, PsycINFO, Pro-Quest, Sage Journals, EBSCOhost, and ScienceDirect. Your school library will usually provide access to these databases as part of your tuition and fees. Academic databases occasionally have non-scholarly articles or reviews, but most have an easy way to restrict your search for *only peer-reviewed* sources. Google Scholar is another option, but again, you need to do your research on the journal that comes up and make sure that it's peer-reviewed.

Going back to Leroy and his research on Haitian trauma, you might recall that he had plagiarized from Encyclopedia Britannica, meaning that Leroy had two strikes against him. Not only had he heavily plagiarized, but he also plagiarized from a non-scholarly source, meaning not only did he need to get rid of the plagiarism in his project, but he also needed to go back to the research stage to obtain acceptable sources.

Use common sense when looking at sources, and if you have any doubts, talk with your classmates, colleagues, or dissertation advisor about your sources and any misgivings you might have. It's better to be overly critical of your sources than not critical enough. Having distinguished the qualities of scholarly sources from those of non-scholarly sources, the next important distinction for conducting research is the differences between *primary* and *secondary* sources.

What Is a Primary Source?

A primary source is any kind of firsthand documentation of an event or action. Eye-witness accounts of events, interviews, autobiographies, letters, and data collected through scientific procedures are all examples of primary sources. If you are writing a historical dissertation, a primary source could be a paper document created by someone in the past (e.g., old letters, diaries, journals, or logbooks). If you are writing a literature dissertation, your primary sources might be poems, novels, or plays. For a dissertation in the social sciences, your primary sources could include responses that people provide to surveys and questionnaires or interview transcriptions. For a dissertation in the hard sciences, your primary sources may be data from experiments or studies. Other kinds of primary sources might include newspaper or magazine articles, maps and artifacts, sound recordings or films, government documents, or interviews. What the different kinds of primary sources have in common is that they are raw data that you can directly analyze and interpret. Even if others have analyzed the same material before, if you are looking at it directly and not through another scholar's summary or interpretation, then it is a primary source.

How Do I Find Primary Sources?

You can find some kinds of primary sources in online databases. If your institution's library subscribes to resources like ProQuest, you can search that database for newspaper and magazine articles. If you don't have access to subscription-based databases, Google News provides free access to back issues of many periodicals. You can find hard copies of primary sources in libraries. Most libraries provide access to hard copies of newspapers and periodicals. Some have recordings of oral history interviews or archival collections that include government documents, letters, diaries, etc. Many libraries post listings or catalogs of their archival collections online. You can, for instance, search the Library of Congress' archival collection using its online catalog; or you can search the Online Archive of California website to look for primary sources at different institutions across California. Some of these sources will be open to the public, while others may require you to request permission. Typically, if you are a student doing doctoral research at an institution, you should not have difficulty gaining access to these materials.

That said, Allen had several colleagues studying history and doing archival research in Egypt and India, who often regaled other members of their cohort with tales of bribery and other measures taken just to gain access to the ancient texts. In one Egyptian archive, Nigel wasn't allowed to make photocopies or photograph the texts. It also cost $50.00/day to enter the archive. He had only ten days to visit the archive, and he knew he wouldn't have enough time to study and translate everything he would need for that chapter of his dissertation, so he actually bought a wristwatch with a secret camera built into it—à la James Bond—to take illegal snapshots of the materials so that he could study them later. While we would *never* suggest that anyone should disobey the rules of a library or archive, sometimes researchers have to go to great lengths to get access to primary sources!

Your institution's library website may have resources for helping you find primary sources. You can also find primary sources in books: look for collections of interviews or anthologies of historical primary sources. Talk to librarians about what primary sources are available to you! Librarians can be a vital source of help as you conduct research. In social sciences and hard sciences, you may end up creating your own primary sources; when you conduct interviews, oral histories, experiments, and studies, you are developing the primary sources that you will use in your dissertation.

How Can Primary Sources Help My Dissertation?

In your dissertation, one of your jobs is to analyze primary sources. To put this another way: your dissertation will tell readers what your primary sources mean and why they are important. If you find primary sources that few (or no) other scholars have analyzed, you'll be able to make a valuable contribution to your discipline. Kara, who was working on her PhD in English at Duke, received funding to do archival research for her literature dissertation in Scotland. While she was there, she came across a novel from 1759 that she thought seemed important, raising important issues of how Scottish nationhood was viewed by and for women, but found that no scholarly work had yet been written on it. She added a chapter on the book to her dissertation, and will be coming out with the first critically-edited version of it with a well-known academic publisher later this year, a wonderful publication item to add to her CV! Even if what you find isn't entirely new, if you can take primary sources that other scholars have used but interpret them in a way that is new and original, your dissertation can be innovative and exciting to other scholars in your field. Using primary sources can thus help you make your mark as a scholar.

What Are Secondary Sources?

Primary sources are, essentially, raw data and information, and the dissertation writer's job is to process that information. Secondary sources are sources in which someone *has analyzed* primary sources or data. Secondary sources include work by other scholars like journal articles, books, and dissertations. They also include nonfiction books and biographies that aren't intended for academic readers, as well as other types of essays or commentaries that describe and analyze primary sources. Secondary sources are the place most people start when conducting background research on their topic. But, as mentioned previously, you must ensure that any secondary sources you include in your dissertation are scholarly.

Finding Books

Once you have a dissertation topic, try using a keyword or subject search in your library catalog to find books related to your topic. Most (if not all) books housed in university libraries qualify as scholarly sources. If you have any doubts, however, check with a librarian or with your advisor before relying too heavily on a questionable source. Once you've used the catalog to locate books that might be useful to you, use their call numbers to locate them on the shelves. Be sure to look at books shelved near the one that you went looking for. Since books are organized according to topic, it's likely that you'll find other useful secondary sources related to your topic that way. Some library online databases have a "browse" function frequently named "see nearby call numbers." When physically browsing the library shelves isn't an option, try browsing virtually whenever possible.

Finding Articles

Databases like Google Scholar and JSTOR are great resources for finding articles. Once you have a dissertation topic, use these sites to search for keywords or subjects related to your topic. A keyword or subject search on these sites will bring up scholarly articles that reference your search terms. You may have to dig through the search results to find the sources most closely related to your dissertation topic. Other places to search for sources are in the reference lists of recent dissertations and articles on topics similar to yours. Using the inverse strategy can also be fruitful. When you find a particularly relevant article, look at who has subsequently cited it (look for a "cited by" or similar link).

When it comes to articles, it's important to consider the publication date. While foundational articles can be used where necessary, it's often optimal or even required by many universities to use a certain percentage of articles published within the past five years. The idea behind this is that articles older than five years will just not be conversant with the most recent developments in your field. Knowing exactly what the parameters are can help you determine the appropriate filters to use in your search. Library databases have a function that will allow you to filter for only peer-reviewed articles published within a certain time period. Be sure to account for your proposed graduation date when setting your parameters. This can save you a lot of pain later in the process, as updating your sources later in the process can be a daunting task.

Literature Review: It's Not an Annotated Bibliography

During graduate school, and especially while you're working on your dissertation, you'll probably hear the terms "annotated bibliography" and "literature review" tossed around a lot. You might know that Chapter 2 of the dissertation is traditionally the Review of the Literature, but it's not necessarily a straight literature review, either; it's a bit more developed, with an introduction, information on search descriptors, and a brief outline of your conceptual/theoretical framework.

So, where does an annotated bibliography fit in, if at all, and how does it differ? While both an annotated bibliography and a literature review are comprehensive collections of sources and research, the two are vastly different.

Elements of an annotated bibliography:

- An ordered list (usually alphabetical) of sources for additional reading, often explaining each source's relevance to the topic, as well as a brief summary
- Each source is listed separately from the other, for easy identification and location
- Each source stands alone and is not integrated with other sources
- Typically points the reader to sources for their own further reading/research

Elements of a literature review:

- Overview of a specific topic with summaries and explanations of the most pertinent and important sources and findings on the subject
- Synthesized, in-depth explanations of the research, integrated into developed paragraphs
- More exploratory than an annotated bibliography, with the aim of presenting a cohesive picture of the existing research
- Sources are discussed together, often compared and contrasted, and discussed in terms of the larger field
- Helps the reader understand the research in a specific way

A literature review is more developed than an annotated bibliography and has a thesis at its core. The literature review chapter in a dissertation should always refer back to your larger project as its focus, not the literature being reviewed. It should highlight why the reader should care about your larger argument and research, and why your thesis statement is so important. By situating your research within a body of literature and identifying the various studies that your research builds upon, confirms, contradicts, or emulates, you give your project credibility and otherwise justify to your reader that this project is well thought out and trustworthy.

An annotated bibliography is merely an expanded list and can be a tool for researching and writing a larger paper. Some schools require annotated bibliographies to be added to larger papers, because they do provide assessments of available research, but are never part of the actual body of the papers.

They are typically an appendix because again, they are a tool to propel you forward to the larger literature review—a building block, if you will. A good annotated bibliography can be helpful for the later development and structure of a literature review. Think of it this way: the annotated bibliography is the framework upon which to build the house of the literature review. By itself, it's just bare beams and studs and you can't tell what it's largely about; it needs connective structures, embellishment, and a good, sturdy foundation.

This is a very important distinction, as many students fall into the trap of conflating the literature review with an annotated bibliography. They will write their literature reviews with each paragraph beginning with the name of an author and simply describe that individual's study. They seek our guidance because their advisor has said their literature review is lacking synthesis, structure, or coherence.

When writing your literature review, it is of paramount importance that it doesn't merely summarize the work you have read. Rather, the literature review situates your research project within various bodies of scholarly literature. Each and every paragraph of your literature review is about your research project. The organization of your literature review should be based on themes, as different aspects of the scholarly conversation are addressed at once. For example, you might have five or six different sources that refer to the efficacy of your chosen methodology. There is no need to separate those out into five or six different paragraphs and address each one individually. Instead, create a paragraph that relates your chosen methodology to those sources and weave between them as you create an argument that justifies why your methodology is appropriate and effective. Thematic organization is one of the most logical ways to construct a literature review chapter. When thinking through your chapter outline, a good place to begin is with the different themes that emerged through your research. Then put them together in an order that makes sense and expand on which sources you will discuss as you tackle each theme. This strategy will result in an engaging chapter that advocates for the significance of your research as it compares to previously conducted studies.

Having reviewed the extant literature, selected scholarly sources and synthesized their significance, you're prepared to make your intervention in the field. Now that you know what hasn't yet been done, it's time to do it! The next chapter includes a discussion of the methodology, results, and discussion chapters you will use to plan, enact, and report on the results of your novel work.

CHAPTER 6

Data: How to Get It, How to Analyze It, How to Present It

Research Questions

You have a general topic for your dissertation, and you've conducted background research to figure out how this topic fits within the larger body of literature. Now, you have to narrow down your research question. Research questions for a dissertation usually consist of a main research question or questions and several sub-questions, which help redirect you in answering the main question(s).

How can you determine what your research questions should be? A good place to start is thinking about the questions that keep coming to mind as you read about and research your topic. Jot those questions down. Often, identifying a gap in the literature can lead you to research questions that are unanswered by the existing literature and therefore worthy of a dissertation. After you have several questions written down, take a critical look at them. Can they be refined into your research questions? Aspects of research questions to consider include:

- Are they clear? Research questions should be as clear as possible and give you explicit direction. If your questions are unclear, your paper will reflect that, and you will likely waste a lot of time with inefficient research on things you don't need for your dissertation.
- Are they specific? You want questions pointed enough to give you direction and enable you to write a dissertation rather than a multivolume tome, but you don't want an overly narrow focus. You want questions that are specific yet complex enough to require research.

In this chapter, we refer to a fictitious study about factors that affect dissertation writers' perceptions of their work-life balance. To start, here is an example of an ineffective research question (RQ), rewritten to be more effective:

Ineffective RQ: What factors affect dissertation writers' work-life balance?

Effective RQ: What, if any, differences in perceived levels of work-life balance exist between dissertation writers who set a specific work schedule and those who do not?

When formulating your research questions, think of open-ended questions (i.e., "how" or "why" questions). Phrase the questions in neutral terms to avoid possible skewing of research or data. You don't want your research questions to be leading. Choose something that fascinates you: a question that *you* actively want to answer! This is important because you'll be studying this for several years, and if you don't like what you're studying, it will be that much harder to motivate yourself to work and make the process a lot less enjoyable.

When you have potential research questions, ask yourself about ethical issues that might arise: What are possible risks/benefits to the researcher or subjects? Will this hurt anyone? Who will it benefit? Can my data be misused to hurt people? Think about whether your research questions are feasible. Is it possible, on a practical level, to do the necessary research for your questions? Would it require an enormous sample size that you just can't get? Are you able to collect the data?

Judith, an EdD candidate at Trident University, planned to ask high school administrators and students to respond to a lengthy questionnaire and then interview each of the administrators and students for an hour. Judith was hoping to interview 100 students and at least a dozen administrators. She was planning to survey and interview far more participants than she needed to reach data saturation. Furthermore, she was giving herself far too much work to review and synthesize. She would need a team of researchers to make such a study feasible, yet all she had was herself. When considering all the work to organize each interview, run the interview, manage the data, dictate the interview, code the data, and then analyze and write about them, each person she interviewed would likely represent ten hours of work. She was giving herself hundreds if not thousands of hours of work when all she needed to do was interview five or six administrators (still a solid couple of weeks of working full-time to incorporate the data into her study properly). She didn't need to have anyone respond to questionnaires, and she didn't need to interview students. What she did need was another set of eyes on her research plan to save her from going overboard.

Alignment

A key to a strong, cohesive dissertation is alignment. There are two main ways in which a dissertation must align. The first is that the research questions must align with the subject matter and the theoretical framework. If the research question is unrelated to the topic, the committee will reject it. To return to the fictional study example, here is an example of a research question that would not be aligned with that topic: Do dissertation writers who set a clearly defined schedule finish faster? This question is not aligned with the topic, because it has to do with the pace of completion and is irrelevant to the dissertation's focus on work-life balance. Here is an example of a question that is aligned with that topic: Does setting a rigid 40-hour workweek contribute to dissertation writers' perceived work-life balance?

The second form of alignment has to do with the relationship between your research questions and your methodology. They have to line up with each other. If they do not, not only will your committee notice and request revisions in this area, but it will also create a chaos of sorts within your paper, especially in terms of writing and organization. As a result, you have to think about methodology when choosing your research questions. Part of creating effective research questions is knowing they can be answered by the methodology you are also selecting.

For example, take the following quantitative research question: What percentage of dissertation writers have a set weekly schedule? If you chose to interview five writers about their schedules, your methodology would not be aligned with your research question. If you chose to distribute a survey to 2,000 dissertation writers about their scheduling preferences, your methodology would be more aligned with your research question. If your research question were qualitative (How do dissertation writers perceive the importance of a weekly schedule?), interviewing five graduate students would be better aligned with your research question.

What Is the Difference Between Qualitative and Quantitative Methodology?

Two main families of methodologies exist: qualitative and quantitative. Qualitative studies seek to understand subjective interrelationships while quantitative studies seek to establish and examine definitive numerical relationships. Most research in the humanities is qualitative, though quantitative studies are possible. Conversely, scientific research is generally quantitative, but qualitative studies may be possible. Researchers in the social sciences may choose between the two approaches or combine them, depending on the goals of their studies. The following table lays out some distinctions between the two types of inquiry:

Qualitative	Quantitative
Investigates and expresses concepts via words	Investigates and expresses concepts via numbers
Asks, "Why? How? What is the context? What are the implications?"	Asks, "How much? How many? What is the strength of the correlation?"
Develops a theory	Tests a theory
Establishes legitimacy by acknowledging its subjectivity and accounting for its own bias	Establishes legitimacy by striving for objectivity and freedom from bias
Interprets	Measures
Values processes over outcome	Values outcome over processes
Requires rich sources	Requires a statistically significant sample size
Assumes dynamic, organic reality about which humans create meaning	Assumes a static, mechanistic, knowable reality
Focuses on narratives, symbols, human interactions, and systems of human meaning	Focuses on facts, statistics, correlation or causation, and numerical relationships
Reasons dialectically and inductively	Reasons logistically and deductively
Explores	Seeks definitive conclusions
Establishes credibility via member check, interview corroboration, peer debriefing, prolonged engagement, negative case analysis, auditability, confirmability, bracketing, and/or balance; generalizations are suspect	Establishes validity via replicable results; seeks results that can be generalized
Claims must be arguable (that is, an equally intelligent, informed researcher could take an opposing viewpoint)	Claims must be falsifiable (that is, evidence that would disprove them must be imaginable)
Seeks culturally specific truths	Seeks universal truths
Methods include interviews and case studies	Methods include empirical observation and measurement

Qualitative methods can be used to develop quantitative research questions or to interpret the results of quantitative studies. Moving back and forth between quantitative and qualitative ways of understanding your dissertation topic during the planning phase may allow you to explain it in richer ways, using words and numbers; it may allow you to see an old problem from a fresh perspective, or it may allow contradictions or disconnections to emerge, leading to new lines of inquiry.

Changing Methodologies

Sometimes students change from a qualitative to a quantitative methodology depending on feasibility. You might set out to conduct interviews and discover that the people you wish to interview aren't as available as you originally thought, and it would be much more feasible to get those people to respond to a survey instead. To revisit Judith (the doctoral candidate whose goal for interviewing participants was far out of scope), she did away with her survey component and her student interview component after discovering that interviewing a student population required many more steps than an adult population. Ultimately, she realized that she would glean more than enough data from the administrator interviews. As you develop your methodologies, you might discover that the survey questions you are creating are too limiting in scope and you want to conduct interviews to have a more open-ended approach. If you do change your research methods, you will need to go back and reframe your research question to fit the new methodology.

Here are three sample research questions that interrogate the same topic—the work-life balance of a doctoral candidate—each using a different methodology:

Qualitative research question: How does a graduate student's writing schedule affect their perceived level of work-life balance?

Quantitative research question: How does a graduate student's writing schedule affect writers' average time to dissertation completion?

Mixed methods research question: How does a dissertation writer's writing schedule affect their perceived level of work-life balance, and how does writing schedule affect writers' average time to dissertation completion?

While these questions are appropriately aligned with a research topic addressing dissertation writers' schedules and their effects on work-life balance and/or completion time, the first is effective for a qualitative researcher seeking to obtain information about what kind of subjective experiences and attitudes the participants have about an aspect of the topic. The second research question would be best used by a quantitative researcher interested in demonstrating variability of dissertation completion time. The last research question, mixed methods, gives us a quantity (quantitative question) to consider, how much time the graduate students will take to finish their degree, and a question about the nature of some type of phenomena (qualitative question): How does this writing schedule affect your work-life balance? Before moving on, make sure that your research question fits with the type of information you aim to discover and how you plan to go about obtaining it.

Lastly, it's important to keep in mind that doctoral projects often have multiple research questions or sub-questions. Each question might be answerable with the same type of data analysis method, or in the case of mixed methods studies, the research questions might require different methods of collecting and analyzing data.

Here are examples of research questions with fully fleshed out sub-questions:

Qualitative

RQ: How does a graduate student's writing schedule affect their perceived level of work-life balance?

Sub-question: How do dissertation writers who follow a set weekly writing schedule describe their work-life balance?

Sub-question: How do dissertation writers, who follow a flexible writing schedule and do not use set hours, describe their work-life balance?

Quantitative

RQ: How does a writing schedule affect writers' average time to dissertation completion?

Sub-question: What is the average length of time to completion among dissertation writers who follow a set weekly writing schedule?

Sub-question: What is the average length of time to completion among dissertation writers who do not follow a set weekly writing schedule?

Mixed Methods

RQ: How does a dissertation writer's writing schedule affect their perceived level of work-life balance and which type of schedule is most commonly adopted?

Sub-question: What percentage of dissertation writers adopt a set writing schedule compared to a flexible writing style?

Sub-question: How do dissertation writers who follow a set weekly writing schedule describe their work-life balance?

Sub-question: How do dissertation writers who follow a flexible writing schedule and do not use set hours describe their work-life balance?

Hypotheses

Now that you have written your research questions, it's time to develop a hypothesis for each of them. There are different types of hypotheses. A null hypothesis is the hypothesis that there will be no statistically significant difference between groups being analyzed. The alternative hypotheses means that the differences will be statistically significant. Referring back to our quantitative study on doctoral students' work-life balance, the following might be some hypotheses we would use to describe the project. After each hypothesis, we have named the statistical test we'd use to answer that research question and prove (or disprove) each of the hypotheses. In a later section, we will discuss common statistical tests and how you might determine which one is appropriate for your project.

RQ1: How Does a Flexible Writing Schedule Relate to Perceived Work-Life Balance?

Null hypothesis: There are no significant differences in reported work-life balance levels between dissertation writers who adopt a flexible schedule and those who adopt set schedules.

Alternate hypothesis: There are significant differences in reported work-life balance levels between dissertation writers who adopt a flexible schedule and those who adopt set schedules.

Analysis: You might run an independent samples t-test to assess for differences in perceived work-life balance levels between dissertation writers who adopt a flexible schedule versus those who adopt set schedules.

RQ2: Do Certain Ranges of Hours Spent Writing per Week Lead to Different Levels of Perceived Work-Life Balance?

Null hypothesis: There are no significant differences between dissertation writers in work-life balance correlated with hours spent writing per week.

Alternate hypothesis: There are significant differences in perceived work-life balance between dissertation writers according to how much time is spent writing per week.

Analysis: You will run a one-way Analysis of Variance (ANOVA) to test for differences in reported work-life balance between dissertation writers who report different ranges of time spent writing per week. This will be followed up with post hoc tests to assess what the differences between each pair are and if they are significant.

Analysis Planning

Once you have identified a gap in the literature worth investigating, pinpointed your research questions, and have chosen the research design you will use to answer these questions (qualitative approach, quantitative approach, or mixed methods design), it's time to move into the analysis planning stage. Your analysis plan will be an integral part of your methodology chapter.

What Is Analysis Planning?

During this stage, you will start to think about how you are going to measure the concepts identified in your research questions and decide which analyses are appropriate to evaluate them. More specifically, the right data analysis method will allow you to assess the specific proposed relationships between these concepts. At this stage, you will start to consider which assumptions about your data need to be met to test these hypothesized relationships and which tests will be necessary to ensure they have been met.

Typically, this process begins by closely examining your research questions and the associated hypothesized relationships. You will then look closely at each concept in your research questions and hypotheses and decide how to measure each of these concepts. For example, if you are interested in exploring well-being, you will need to determine how best to measure well-being (this might be a combination of several questionnaires). If you are looking to explore gender, you will need to decide—before you begin data collection—how you are going to measure that concept.

Once you have collected your data, you will need to assign variables (and groups of variables) to each concept you use in your hypotheses/research questions, ensuring you have all the data you need to answer your research questions. It is better to have a clear idea of how you will match these up before you begin collecting data to avoid a heartbreaking scenario where you realize you have not asked the correct questions to adequately answer your hypotheses/research questions.

Finally, during the analysis planning stage, you will need to determine exactly which statistical tests are necessary/ideal to test your hypotheses. In the next section, you'll find a list of common tests and how they are used. This can be a starting point for figuring out how to analyze your data; however, if you are lost, be sure to ask an expert for help!

Why Is It Important?

The analysis plan is typically included in the methods chapter of your dissertation and is essential to ensuring that you can test your research questions/hypotheses with confidence. It is crucial that you explain clearly and confidently how you chose the variables to match the concepts you identified in your research questions, why you chose the statistical tests you used, and whether your data matched the required assumptions for each statistical test *before* you defend your dissertation project.

Common Quantitative Analysis Tests Used in Social Science Research

Here's a list of many of the most common tests we see at Dissertation Editor. This is by no means an exhaustive list and certainly there are plenty of students working in other areas.

However, the following list should provide a basis for introducing the most common analyses used in the social sciences.

Correlation Analyses

Correlation analyses are used to measure the strength and direction of the association between two or more variables. For example, if you are interested in exploring whether time spent outdoors is significantly associated with severity of depression and you wish to determine the strength of the relationship, as well as the direction of the relationship (positively or negatively associated), this is the statistical test for you. However, this test does not tell you which variable causes the other.

T-tests

A t-test is used to determine whether there is a significant difference in mean scores (of some measurement/instrument) between two groups. There are two types: paired samples t-test used to measure changes in the same group across time and independent samples t-test used to measure changes in different groups. For example, if you want to explore whether mean scores on a cognitive task significantly change after a mindfulness intervention, you might choose to run a paired samples t-test to compare mean scores before the intervention to mean scores after the intervention. If you want to explore whether mean scores on a cognitive task significantly differ between those who practice meditation versus those who do not, you might choose to run an independent samples t-test to test group differences.

Chi-square Tests

When you are interested in whether there is a significant relationship between two groups and your variables of interest are categorical in nature, the chi-square test is appropriate. For example, a researcher who wants to explore whether there is a significant relationship in their sample population—such as, whether participants' choice to work in a specific industry has any correlation with their marital status—a chi-square test analysis would be appropriate.

ANOVA

Analysis of Variance (ANOVA) tests are used to determine whether there are significant differences in mean scores (of some measurement/instrument) between three or more groups. For example, if you wish to determine whether there are significant differences in time spent outdoors between urban, rural, and suburban populations, you might choose an ANOVA test.

Linear Regression Analysis

Linear regression analysis is used to determine the extent to which a continuous independent variable can predict the value of a dependent variable. For example, a researcher who wanted to determine if the amount of time one spends outdoors can predict scores on a depression measure would choose to use a linear regression analysis.

Factor Analysis

Factor analysis is used to determine exactly which interrelated factors represent a broader, more complex concept, as well as to determine the extent to which items contribute to each factor. For example, if a researcher wants to develop a new measure to explore participants' beliefs about motherhood, that researcher might conduct a factor analysis to determine which interrelated sub-factors are representative of this broader concept.

Statistical Significance

Statistical significance is not a measure of a research project's worth or value. It's a specific term used to describe the results of a study. It indicates the likelihood that the effect found occurred by chance. For example, Lupe, a student in south Texas, wanted to explore a common belief that Latinas possess a higher level of body acceptance than their White counterparts; they are not so driven by the "thin ideal" and are comfortable in rounder, lusher figures. Thus, they are not as prone to anorexia, bulimia, and unhealthy calorie restriction. Lupe, a Latina herself, decided to demonstrate this phenomenon empirically by surveying female students at her south Texas university, which has almost equal numbers of Latinx and White students. She chose to use a p-value, or significance value, of 0.05. That means that there would be a 5 percent chance that the results of her study could occur if the null hypothesis was true. Her literature review and previous research supported the popular conception that Latinas accept fuller body types. She used a well-established body image measure, the Body Appreciation Scale (BAS-2), and gathered 500 responses from women ranging from freshmen to seniors in college.

After doing an independent samples t-test to compare White and Latina responses, Lupe called her advisor to say that her dissertation project was a failure: "I didn't find anything!" she mourned. The t-test turned out nonsignificant, suggesting that there was no difference between the groups. Dr. Lopez, her advisor, reassured her that a finding of "no significance" is not at all a failure. Finding no difference when you really expect one is meaningful in itself. Lupe's somewhat surprising results were cause for logical speculation that could be developed in her discussion chapter. For example, by the time a Latina is a student at a large public university, she may be just as brain-washed into the "thin ideal" as any other woman. Or women who go to college may be different in this regard from women who stay near home after high school. Or the college students could consist of mostly second- and third-generation citizens, who are likely to embrace mainstream values rather than the values of their predecessors. Lupe thought about what research projects could explore the veracity of these speculations and proposed such research in the future directions section of her discussion chapter.

Lupe successfully defended her dissertation and, with Dr. Lopez's help, revised it as an article for publication. They suffered a few rejections from diversity-focused publications, which they suspected was due to these publications' commitment to studies showing differences rather than similarities. At a well-regarded general psychological services journal, however, they received an acceptance with very few revisions. The article was published, and a highlight of Lupe's vita is her achievement of an important publication even before she graduated. "Just because a statistic is nonsignificant doesn't mean it's not significant!" she now asserts.

Qualitative Analysis Planning

While quantitative analysis tends to use specific tests, qualitative analysis starts with coding and reviewing the available data. When you're planning your qualitative study, you want to make sure your interview questions are focused on what concepts you want to measure in your population of interest. Once your data is collected, the coding process takes a few iterations before clear themes emerge. This coding process can be understood as tagging your text data, which can then be used to generate variables. You may want to decide early on if you're going to create this coding scheme by consulting the data or by basing it on a theoretical framework in your discipline.

Once your coding scheme is developed, the analysis can range from being descriptive to establishing conceptual relationships. This can include aspects like extracting relevant quotes or creating a code cross-tabulation matrix to explore associations. It will really depend on the research questions you are trying to answer.

Writing Your Methodology Chapter

The methodology section of your dissertation is where you describe what you did and how you did it. Don't let the term "methodology" scare you—it's really just a fancy way of saying method. This section is where you outline the plan that you followed and the steps that you took in completing your research. During the proposal phase of a dissertation, this chapter is typically written in the future tense. Once the proposal has been accepted, the student will convert it to past tense and make any adjustments that might have resulted in altering the methodology during the data collection phase. This section is important to your dissertation because it shows your reader how you went about finding your results. In outlining your methodology, you'll demonstrate that you've used legitimate scholarly methods. It's one of the places in your dissertation where you show what you learned to do in graduate school: to conduct research like a scholar! If you used new or innovative methods in completing your dissertation research, this is where you tell your reader about them. It's your chance to demonstrate how you've contributed to the way that scholars in your field conduct research.

In some fields or departments, you may be expected to devote an entire chapter to describing and justifying your methodology.

In other fields, there may be less of an emphasis on methodology. You may briefly describe your methods in a few pages of your introduction or first chapter. Your dissertation advisor can offer guidance on how extensive your methodology section needs to be.

For a dissertation in the social sciences involving human subject research, you should describe the context or setting of your study (i.e., when and where you conducted your research), who participated in the study, what instruments or methods you used to collect data, and what procedures you used to complete your study and analyze your data. For other kinds of dissertations, your methodology section might be different. In a literature dissertation, for instance, your methodology section might outline which texts you are analyzing and explain what theoretical perspective informs your analysis. It's best to consult with your dissertation advisor about what is appropriate or necessary for your dissertation.

Institutional Review Board (IRB)

You've finished your proposal, and now it's time to collect data and conduct your research. But wait: first, you have to get IRB approval. Many students are often surprised by this or are unclear as to what the IRB is and why it creates this hurdle that must be crossed prior to conducting research.

What Is It?

The IRB is an administrative group that protects the rights and well-being of human research subjects who participate in research projects, whether in the context of schools, hospitals, or other institutions. The IRB makes sure that human subjects in research studies have their welfare and rights protected and that their identities remain private. Each school may be slightly different, but generally there is a process for obtaining IRB approval for your specific study that will ensure your research meets all regulations, including those of your educational institution and federal regulations.

The IRB is generally composed of at least five individuals, all from different backgrounds. This is to ensure a diverse amount of experience and input regarding the implications of your proposed study. There is also at least one IRB member who is not affiliated with the institution and one member who is not a scientist. Consultants also work with the IRB. In addition to approving or rejecting proposals, the IRB may conduct periodic checks to ensure researchers are following the protocol laid out in their IRB application.

Why Is It Important?

Many of you might have heard about some of the unethical research done in the past (Stanford Prison Experiment, anyone?). This board was created to protect the rights and welfare of human research participants to ensure they are treated ethically.

Tips for Making Sure You Pass

When writing your proposal for your IRB application, you should be aware of several elements the IRB is looking for. Addressing each of the points below with care and attention to detail will improve your chances of obtaining approval.

1. As the researcher, it is your responsibility to protect the privacy of your participants' data. When writing your proposal, be clear about how you plan to maintain confidentiality of

participants' personal information. You will want to explain how you are going to make sure participants' names (and/or other personal information) are kept separate from their data. You will need to explain how you will keep all of the data and other personal information about the participants stored in a safe/locked location and explain how (and when) you will properly dispose of their data, once the study has been completed. Hint: you'll usually need to keep data for three years and then dispose of it.

2. It is your responsibility to ensure your participants are participating in the research study of their own free will and that they know exactly what to expect. This includes telling participants—using very plain and straightforward language—about whether there are any risks involved in participating in the study, how they can withdraw from the study at any time with no negative consequences, and explaining to them how their data will be used and protected. And all of these explanations must be provided to participants before they take part in the study. These points are typically written in a detailed informed consent form, which each participant must read and sign before taking part in the study. Be sure to save an unsigned informed consent form, as you will want to include it as an appendix in your dissertation.

3. It is up to you to minimize risk in your study. You should demonstrate that you have considered any risk/potential harm to which your participants

may be subject while participating in your study and that you have reduced any risk/potential harm to the best of your ability. If your research requires an element of risk that may be potentially harmful to the participant, the risk/potential harm needs to be thoroughly and thoughtfully justified in your application.

Writing Your Results

Goal of a Results Chapter

The main goal of a results chapter—typically Chapter 4 in a standard five-chapter dissertation—is to present the results of your data analyses in the most clear, concise, and thorough way possible. One way to achieve the most straightforward, concise report of your results is through tables, graphs, and figures, which should be supplemented by a write-up explaining the most important aspects (rather than the whole table/figure/graph). If you have conducted qualitative research, this chapter will include direct quotes from interviews with your participants. Whether you have conducted qualitative or quantitative research, this is where you tell your reader what you discovered: not the significance or interpretation of what you discovered, just the facts.

What's Included

In your results chapter, present any quantitative information about your participants. These are called descriptive statistics, which let the reader know who your participants are, including information about their age, gender, education, race, etc. In addition to reporting on the socio-demographics of your participants, you should explore whether there are any differences between groups and account for any confounding variables related to participant demographics, attrition, or other potential factors that could be overlooked.

Answer each of your research questions concisely in this chapter, preferably in the order you presented them in previous chapters (keep it consistent throughout!). Make it clear to the reader which analyses you used to test your hypotheses, report the tests of assumptions for each analysis you have run, and then present the results, including whether your hypotheses were rejected or accepted. If you aren't sure whether you should include certain results, go back to your research questions, re-read them, and decide whether the results are relevant to your questions. If so, then include them. If not, then don't.

Another thing to think about is how best to present your results, and whether it's best to include figures, graphs, text, or tables. A variety of formats can keep the results section interesting and fresh for the reader. At the same time, you don't want to overwhelm the reader visually and make the chapter appear choppy or sloppy. You only need to include tables, graphs, and figures if they make the results easier to understand. If you choose to use tables, graphs, and figures, use them sparingly and wisely, caption them well, and introduce them and the content in them to the reader before you present them. For more on this topic, see the section on "Putting Visual Aids in Your Dissertation."

What's Not Included

Do not discuss your chosen methodology in this chapter, nor how the results relate to the literature in your field or your theoretical framework. Both of these are covered in other chapters and are not pertinent to this one. There is no need to go into detail about the variables you have used in this chapter or the past literature on these variables. Keep this chapter focused on objectively reporting the results; this will result in tighter writing and a more credible, academic tone.

Writing Your Discussion Section

Goal of This Chapter

The goal of the discussion chapter is to reflect, thoughtfully, on the results of your analyses and explain systematically to the reader how the results of your analyses relate to your research questions and to the literature in your field. The goal of the discussion chapter is for the researcher to explore and reflect on whether their findings are in line with previous research in the field and also to demonstrate how their findings are new and unique, emphasizing how the new findings contribute to the field. It is important to highlight the impact of your findings to the reader in this chapter.

What's Included

The limitations and delimitations are discussed in this chapter. The limitations that you should present include factors that may have influenced the results that you were not able to control. The delimitations should also be presented, informing the reader about the decisions you made that may have restricted your study or findings. The difference between limitations and delimitations is often a stumbling block for students, but the key is whether they were outside your control (limitations) or within your control (delimitations). For example, unexpectedly being unable to conduct in-person interviews due to a pandemic is a *limitation*; the choice to select your participants to individuals who defended their dissertation between March 2020 and March 2022 to see how the COVID-19 pandemic affected their dissertation completion process is a *delimitation.*

You'll also present your findings (again, preferably in the same order you presented your research questions and results for consistency) and discuss how they relate to the existing literature in your field, with an emphasis on how your findings are unique and what they add to the field. Any potential impact of your findings should be explored and discussed, along with suggestions and directions for future research.

What's Not Included

The discussion chapter, like the other chapters in your dissertation, serves a specific purpose. Therefore, in this chapter, you do not include information on what methods you chose and used, which analyses were conducted, or statistical test results. These are all addressed in other chapters.

Writing Your Conclusion

You're almost done with your dissertation or thesis, but there's still that pesky conclusion chapter. Frequently, the discussion and conclusion are combined in one, final, fifth chapter; however, many programs separate them out into separate chapters. Whether it is a stand-alone chapter or the final section of chapter five, the conclusion of your dissertation is not simply a short and fast summary—it can be the most powerful, important part of your dissertation. It is the last thing your readers will absorb, and you want it to be strong to have the greatest impact on the reader. Writing a good conclusion chapter is more than mere regurgitation of what's already been said, so read on to find out how to make your conclusion count.

What Are the Goals of the Conclusion Chapter?

Before you begin, it's good to know what you're aiming for. So, let's look at the main goals of the conclusion chapter.

- Provide an overview of your original research and contributions to the field from the paper and how they fit into the larger research on the topic
- Summarize the major points from your previous chapters and key findings
- Make recommendations based on your findings and any limitations you've discovered
- Provide suggestions for future research on the topic

What Should You NOT Do in Your Conclusion Chapter?

There are also some things you should not do in your conclusion chapter, such as:

- Introduce new material or findings
- Overwrite or go over every single finding you've already discussed
- Ignore any of your research questions
- Repeat anything you have already explained in your discussion chapter

Make sure your conclusion chapter addresses everything you set out to explore before wrapping everything up.

Things to Keep in Mind

An important quality of the conclusion chapter is your ability, as a researcher, to reflect on your work both creatively and thoughtfully. Think of it this way: If someone were to read *only* the conclusion chapter of your dissertation, what should they know about your most salient points? What would you want them to take away from your work? You can be more specific and subjective here about what your dissertation contributes to the field and what you have deduced from your work.

Adding Visual Aids to Your Dissertation

Visual aids, like tables and figures, can provide the reader with necessary information quickly and clearly. However, if you have too many unnecessary tables or figures, they can interrupt the flow of the paper and become an annoying distraction to the reader. The key is to use them wisely and appropriately.

What Is the Purpose of Tables and Figures in a Scholarly Paper?

Tables and figures help the reader understand information in your paper and can help provide clarity with your data and results. To clarify the difference between tables and figures: Tables convey data in the form of numbers and text, typically aligned in rows and columns; and figures convey data using images. These can be photographs; flow charts; bar, line, or pie graphs; or just about any other kind of visual representation of information. Often, students are uncertain about whether they have inserted a table or a figure, as we frequently see them mislabeled. The simplest way to think about it is if it's only got numbers and text, it's probably a table. If it has anything else, it's probably a figure. Before putting a table or figure into your paper, here are some things to consider:

- <u>Is this necessary?</u> The point of a visual aid is to communicate information quickly and clearly, not to take up space or complicate things. Simple descriptive statistics can easily be put into the text and don't need a table. Data in a table that requires two or fewer columns should just be placed into the text.
- <u>Relation to text.</u> Tables and figures complement and supplement the text, so the text should refer to the visual aid and mention what the reader should note. The table or figure should be placed near said text. It can be frustrating to read a document in which the author is continually referring to graphics that are far away from their reference in the text. When tables and figures are far away from the text that mentions them, the reader has to flip around from page to page trying to find the relevant visual aid and then flip back to find where they were in the article. Put simply, keep it together. Similarly, always refer to a table or figure by its number (i.e., "see Table 4," rather than "see the table below"). Position on the page can change during manuscript formatting, so it's always better to be specific.
- <u>Cite appropriately.</u> If you are borrowing a table, figure, or visual piece of data from another source, make sure you have all of the information from said source to cite it properly. If you use a table or figure from another source, it should be replicated exactly, then cited per the appropriate formatting style. Different fields and universities have different stipulations about what constitutes academic fair use. Confer with your advisor and/or graduate student

handbook to determine whether you need to seek permission from the copyright holder to use a table or figure in your work.

- <u>Be consistent</u>. Tables and figures should be numbered sequentially; probability values and abbreviations should be consistent, as should titles and formatting. Always use the same spacing. Columns and rows should be labeled similarly, and the data should be aligned the same way.
- <u>Do not repeat data in multiple tables or figures</u>. Each visual aid should have unique information.
- <u>Recreate tables from SPSS or other statistical programs</u>. While it's tempting to simply insert the ready-made table, these often contain way too much information that isn't necessary for the reader. Decide what is pertinent and create a new table.
- <u>Choose unique figures</u>. Similarly, for figures, it is important that the information in the figure be unique, not repeated, and easily understandable. It might be tempting to insert every histogram generated during your analysis; however, it is important not to clutter your dissertation with unnecessary graphics.

Titles, Captions, and Proper Formatting

Each academic formatting style has specific rules for how tables and figures are labeled. All formatting styles require a title and caption for each visual aid. In APA 7th Edition style, the titles and captions of tables and figures always appear above the visual aid. The table/figure number comes first and should be in bold text. The title of the table/figure should be placed one line underneath in italics and is not bold. Tables should not be shaded, nor should they have any vertical lines separating the columns. When a table breaks across pages, you don't need to insert "continued" or the title again, but you do need to repeat the first header row on the second page of the table. See Table 1 and Figure 1 for examples of these elements in APA format.

Table 1

Summary of Descriptions of Level of Work-Life Balance by Graduate Students With Set Writing Schedules (n = 162)

Categories	# of Comments	Selected Examples of Comments
Excellent	17	Structure keeps me on track, and I love having a set schedule. I write from 6am–11am and noon to 3pm every weekday, and keep a list of dissertation-related tasks other than writing (research, reference list cleanup, etc.) beside my computer in case I'm having trouble working on a particular section. I find that treating the dissertation as my 9–5 job means that I can close my computer and enjoy the evening with my partner.
Good	62	For the most part, I love having a set schedule. It gives me discipline and structure, and helps my family understand that writing my dissertation is my work. I do find that sometimes I have the best ideas at hours when I'm not supposed to be working, so I keep a journal around the house to jot down notes at those times, but try not to sit down to my computer otherwise.
Fair	35	A set schedule worked extremely well for me when I was working on my master's thesis, so I decided to do the same with my dissertation. But I had a baby during my PhD coursework, and now, my set schedule means that I'm both missing optimal work windows during naptimes and at odd hours of the night, and feeling guilty for working when the baby is awake. I might need to pivot to a more flexible approach.

Categories	# of Comments	Selected Examples of Comments
Poor	18	I'd hoped that adopting a rigid schedule would help me disconnect from my work at the end of the day, but it just means that I actually end up working more. I spend a lot of my set hours staring at a blank Word document, then wake up in the middle of the night thinking about my dissertation.

Figure 1
Pie Chart Showing Percentage of Dissertation Writers Interviewed for This Study Who Adopted a Set Writing Schedule vs. a Flexible Writing Schedule

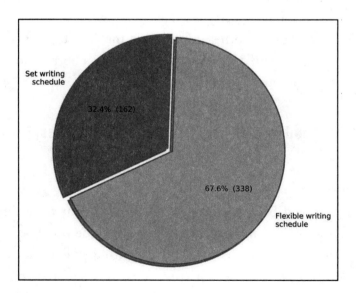

Note. Numbers inside parentheses in each of the wedges reports absolute number of interviewee responses for each category. Total number of interview participants = 500.

A Note About Notes

While not every table or figure needs a note, there are some instances where it's necessary:

- If your table is taken from an outside source, provide a note that it's "reprinted from" or "adapted from" another source. Then, cite the publication information for the original source in the appropriate formatting style. As mentioned before, check with your department to determine if permissions are necessary.
- You should specify p-values in a note.
- If there's any other information that you feel is necessary, or if you need to explain an abbreviation, add a note to the table or figure.

Academic Styles: Citations, References, Footnotes, and Endnotes

Overview

Before you begin writing or researching your dissertation, make sure you know which academic style guide you'll be using. Different disciplines use different formatting styles, which can be confusing. While many specific styles are associated with disciplines (APA with psychology, MLA with literature, Chicago Manual of Style with history, etc.), and universities usually provide graduate students with requirements for which to use, sometimes, which style guide to use is left up to the dissertation writer. In either case, waiting to select a style guide until you get to the reference list will lead to a huge headache. As well as references, style guides provide guidance that you'll need throughout the writing process, like how to format in-text citations, how to write numbers, and which writing style is appropriate. As such, be sure to check with your advisor/university and decide on which style guide you'll be using as early in the process as you can.

Basics of APA Reference Format

APA is the style of the American Psychological Association and is used for many dissertations across fields, especially in education and the social sciences. Because APA is often more scientifically focused than other styles and emphasizes the importance of up-to-date research, it foregrounds the publication year of sources. In your text, if you're using APA style, you'll provide authors' last names and year of publication with in-text citations, presented in parentheses. In the reference list, you'll provide a full entry for all sources you cited in the text. With APA in particular, it's important to conduct a "reference audit" to make sure that every source cited in your paper is listed in the references, and every source listed in the references is cited in your paper. This is one of the time-consuming but crucial tasks a professional editor can help with to save you significant time and stress.

The American Psychological Association released the 7th Edition of its manual in the fall of 2019. By the time of this publication, it has become the standard. Some of the major differences from the 6th Edition include:

- In-text citations: In APA 7, in-text citations of sources with three or more authors should be referred to with the first author's last name followed by et al., even the first time a work is cited (instead of listing up to five authors on first reference).

- <u>Subheadings</u>: APA 7's level 3 subheading is flush left, bold italic, and title case (formerly, this was indented and ended with a period).
- <u>DOI usage</u>: In reference lists, APA 7 requires the DOI to be in full URL link form (https://doi.org/) rather than only listed as a number.

Basics of Chicago Manual of Style

Chicago style (abbreviated CMoS) is generally associated with humanities subjects, specifically history, as well as trade publications. Turabian is similar to Chicago style: it's a simplified form of Chicago style designed for academic works like theses and dissertations. Both are put out by the University of Chicago Press, and most of the formatting elements are the same. The CMoS tends to be more publishing-oriented, whereas Turabian focuses on research papers and academic work. Some programs use the terms interchangeably, so it's best to ask specifically which formatting style you're following, and what kind of citations are expected.

There are two types of documentation used in Chicago style: author-date and notes/bibliography. Chicago author-date style is similar to APA, in that it includes in-text citations with (as the name suggests) the author and the date as well as a reference list. In Chicago notes/bibliography style, the sources are cited as footnotes instead of in the text itself. Chicago style footnotes include all publication information, rather than just the author and date, the first time the work is cited, then a shortened citation thereafter. Note that the previous version of Chicago format used to use the term "Ibid." for a footnote citing the same source as the previous footnote, but now shortened citations are required instead. All sources cited in the text correspond with a footnote. Unlike in APA, a Chicago style bibliography at the end of the text should include all the sources cited but can also list works that you don't cite directly but that helped inform your thoughts on the topic. The most current version of CMoS is the 17th edition (2017), which includes new material on metadata and citation guidelines for an increased range of online sources and other source types.

Other Commonly Used Styles and Resources on How to Use Them

There are many other academic style guides as well. Scholars in the humanities, especially subjects like comparative literature, criticism, or English, often use MLA style (developed by the Modern Language Association). Bluebook is the most widely used legal citation style and is used by most law schools for academic work. Bluebook does not include guidelines on manuscript formatting but does provide guidance for how to cite legal precedents, court cases, and other legislative materials. The AMA style, developed by the American Medical Association, is generally used for scholarly articles for health or medical journals or dissertations in the medical field. The ASA (American Sociological Association) style is typically used in the field of sociology to help students and authors prepare papers and manuscripts for ASA journals and other publications. Other style guides used less frequently include Vancouver, Institute of Electrical and Electronics Engineers (IEEE), the Oxford Standard for Citation of Legal Authorities (OSCOLA), Harvard, and the Modern Humanities Research Association (MHRA).

While the number of and differences between the style guides can feel daunting, resources are available to help you. Each style guide is associated with a publication that provides guidance on all aspects of the style. These often have an online as well as a print version. While these generally require a paid subscription, check to see whether your university library has access to a copy. There are also several free online resources that provide information on multiple style guides. However, be sure to check that you're getting online resources from a reliable source. Those associated with university libraries and writing centers are generally a good bet, while citation generators/less professional resources like EasyBib are not as reliable. The Purdue OWL (the website of their online writing lab) is especially trustworthy.

Citation Software Systems: Pros, Cons, and an Overview of Options

To help with managing what will probably be the longest list of references you've ever worked with, some writers elect to use software programs that manage citations and generate bibliographies. For a long and often unwieldy project like writing a dissertation, it is extremely helpful to use a referencing system that stores your references and makes it easier for you to input citations into your dissertation. At the end of months—and sometimes years—of research, a software program just might save your sanity. Two primary software systems of this type include EndNote and Zotero. After you import the software to your word processor (usually MS Word), you can select which citation style you prefer and import references easily as you write. At the end of your dissertation, you can either manually or automatically generate a properly formatted bibliography. Another helpful feature is that your references, whether parenthetical or footnotes, will be synchronized with your final bibliography. If at any point you delete a reference within the manuscript, it will be deleted automatically from the bibliography as well.

While these tools can be extremely helpful in your dissertation process, they should be used with caution. They have some cons (like software updates), the need to pay for upgrades, and the fact that you'll need to import your references' publication information meticulously into the relevant fields to make sure your reference entries are generated accurately. You'll need to be willing to double-check that you've imported the information for your citations and reference entries correctly to ensure complete accuracy and alignment with your chosen style guide. Most students tend to love or hate these software platforms. You may be unwilling to put in the time and effort it would take for the software to generate error-free reference lists consistently. However, many PhD students could not imagine writing scholarship without these powerful tools. We like to imagine those individuals must have very tidy closets and sock drawers as well.

Now that all required elements are included in your dissertation draft, you can move to the process of revision and move swiftly toward finishing your dissertation. The next chapter addresses the revision and editing process, including a discussion of whether to hire an editor, as well as a description of the defense and final submission processes.

CHAPTER 7

Final Hurdles: Completing and Defending Your Dissertation

Editing and Revisions

Benefits of an Outside Editor

As a graduate student, you likely do not have a ton of disposable income—or any—and so you're careful about how you spend your money. At first, it might seem like a professional editor is a luxury expense that you don't really need, but it can be quite the opposite: a practical expense that can save you lots of time and money in the long run.

An Editor Can Help You Be More Efficient

A professional editor provides personalized, specific feedback on your writing style, strengths and weaknesses, subject matter, and content. This level of personalization is designed with your particular goals in mind. This keeps you from wasting time with generalized platitudes that might not be what you really need. Time is money, and particularly if you're paying each semester to keep working on your dissertation, a professional editor can help you reach your end goal faster, therefore cutting down on tuition expenses.

An Editor Can Help Relieve Stress and Subsequently Increase Your Productivity

It's not a secret that dissertations and theses cause stress, and while multiple revisions and submissions are standard, this can be incredibly stressful and time-consuming. Stress can cause depression, anxiety, and even writing paralysis. If you're pressed for time, those stress effects can add to the pressures you're feeling. A professional editor can help you decipher and address comments from your committee and help you prioritize and focus on the major things you have to work on, saving you a lot of anxiety. Often, as a dissertation writer who has been looking at the same project for a long time, you're simply too close to the subject to see it clearly and objectively assess the next steps you need to take. An editor can also assist you with proper formatting (like applying styles in MS Word, generating a table of contents, troubleshooting page numbers, and citing obscure types of references correctly), which is a major source of stress and anxiety for many students.

You'll Be Able to Reach Your Career Goals Faster

Many students are pursuing a graduate degree for career gains: to get a better job, change employers, or reach the next pay grade. Having to revise and resubmit repeatedly for multiple semesters can delay or derail your career plans. Professional editors can help minimize the number of times you have to resubmit, helping you to finish your degree and reach your career goals in a timely way.

While peer editing can be valuable and certainly has its place, it's hard to find a substitute for a professional editor. Professional editors have years of experience, in-depth knowledge of English grammar, expert writing and editing skills, and thorough knowledge of multiple style guides. Unless your peer is a professional editor, it will be hard for them to equal the services of professional editing and formatting. Similarly, university writing centers can serve as a great resource. However, their consultants are trained not to be directive or do any of the work for you. While we don't write content for clients working on material for school credit (as that wouldn't be ethical), a professional editor can be much more active in revising your writing for you than a university writing consultant, helping decrease your workload.

Regardless of how you get your writing edited, everyone knows it can be very difficult to edit your own writing. The dissertation process means that you necessarily get very close to your chosen subject and spend a great deal of time with your ideas and the writing in your dissertation. It can be easy to get so close to the dissertation that it's hard to make any cuts to it, even if you know it's necessary, and objectivity can be thin on the ground. Working with an editor—whether they are a friend, family member, colleague, or professional—is an integral part of the writing process for any serious work and should not be overlooked or underestimated. Good writing takes time, practice, and help.

Revision

Revision involves looking at something anew—to see it again but from a different perspective. Students are often disappointed when instructed by advisors to revise and resubmit. The need to keep working on a draft is often perceived as failure, when the truth is revision is an integral part of the learning process.

By going back over your writing, reshaping your paragraphs, and reorganizing your thoughts, you can clarify your ideas while also developing new ones. When Allen first started writing his dissertation, he sat down and wrote a chapter that turned out to be 20,000 words long in the first draft. After revising it, reorganizing thoughts, and fleshing out ideas, Allen turned that one chapter into three 10,000-word chapters that were much more eloquent, effective, and efficient.

Marc had written a thematically organized dissertation about the representation of Black women in American theater produced between 1924 and 1984. Initially, he organized it thematically, according to the formal qualities of the plays studied: one on comedies, one on dramas, and one on postmodernism. He had completed a full draft but felt that his ideas weren't hanging together. He had tried to make a crucial point about how the complexity of these representations ebbed and flowed over time, in relation to political and civil rights developments.

Marc spent weeks reviewing the conclusions to each of his chapters, trying to make his points stronger and more eloquent, but it didn't seem to make much of a difference. He then returned to some of the theory and philosophy texts he'd read to develop his conceptual framework, but nothing there lead him toward strengthening his argument either. One day, he met a friend completing a dissertation in a different field for coffee. Conversation turned to the problems they were experiencing in their dissertation, and his friend (an art history PhD candidate) made an offhand comment about his chronological, geographical structure: "I've organized it into the time periods and locations of Van Gogh's career, but I'm having a hard time figuring out how to place general, thematic commentary on interior spaces when they are relevant to both the Paris and Arles chapters."

As soon as Marc returned to his apartment, he printed his entire dissertation, one paragraph to a page (another friend of his, who was completing her dissertation on climate change, later chastised him for this), and organized them according to material that related individual play texts. He then separated them into decades, wrote up a new outline, and started copy/pasting text around his document (electronically this time, to be more environmentally friendly). Much more quickly than he anticipated, he had a new draft of an organization based on a chronological organizational scheme. Of course, new transitions were needed throughout, the introduction had to be revised, and he had trouble fitting some of the old sections into the new structure. But on the whole, the new organizational system provided a more effective framework for Marc's ideas, and the rest of the revision process flowed more naturally.

There are two key takeaways from the story of Marc's revision process. First, sometimes a seemingly huge revision makes the process run more smoothly. Even though a thematic reorganization is a huge undertaking, it was less effort than all the dead ends Marc had tried before his friend's fresh perspective led him in a chronological direction. Second, and crucially, the exact words of your first (or even your fourteenth) draft, are not the be-all-end-all of your ideas. Even if things change drastically as you revise your dissertation, it doesn't mean that anything is lost in terms of your research, ideas, hard effort, or contribution to the knowledge in your field.

The Importance of Proofreading

During the dissertation writing process, a final proofread before submitting to your committee is crucial. Proofreading focuses on spotting and correcting superficial errors of grammar, spelling, diction, syntax, formatting, and punctuation. It's inevitable that there will be one typo in your dissertation—just as there will be in this book. We'll try our best to minimize that and at least make sure it's not on the first page. This is in contrast with editing, which typically takes a more in-depth approach to sentence structure, ideas, arguments, diction, tone, flow, and organization. Proofreading is often one of the last steps before submitting your work, after all of the editing, revising, and rewriting is done. I've found two tactics for proofreading your own work to be particularly effective. First, reading the text out loud can help you catch errors you might not notice while reading through the document quietly. The effort of articulating each word helps highlight areas of awkwardness that make you stumble and removes the tendency to skim, letting your brain move more quickly than your eyes. The second strategy is reading the manuscript backward (paragraph by paragraph or sentence by sentence). This can help remove you from the flow and meaning of the argument and help you consider the words themselves, rather than the ideas to which they relate.

It is often better to have someone other than yourself proofread your paper. Once you have looked at your paper and your content for so many hours a day and for however many months and/or years, it becomes very difficult to catch small but obvious mistakes. An editor can also catch things a simple spell/grammar check cannot. For example, if you've spelled a word correctly but it's the wrong version of the word, a spell-check might not pick that up, but an editor will. If a sentence still doesn't flow right or doesn't convey your intended meaning, an editor will make surface fixes during proofreading. An editor will also be able to identify and correct formatting errors in the document, while a spell-check cannot.

Use caution, as well, with tools like Grammarly. While that type of software certainly has a place, we find that many students treat it as the end-all-be-all of good writing and are gravely disappointed when a document that's already been edited by a human returns with flagged issues after being run through the program. Our recommendation is that, if you're going to use Grammarly or other AI editing software, do so as part of an earlier stage in the revision process, *then* move to human proofreading. While it is undeniably smart, software still can't do what humans can, and often has difficulty with key aspects of good APA-style writing, like removing anthropomorphism or ensuring scholarly tone.

Proofreading isn't just confined to the dissertation or thesis process. When you write a business memo, professional paper, conference poster presentation, or business email, doing a quick proofread of your writing can help you catch embarrassing spelling errors (thanks, autocorrect!) or glaring mistakes. Taking the extra minute or two for proofreading, for even these smaller documents, can mean the difference between appearing polished and professional or disorganized and harried.

Final Formatting

Dissertation formatting can be a beast in and of itself. Many students have written extensive compelling research culminating years of experience in one magnum opus, only to get completely flummoxed by automating their table of contents and getting the page numbers to shift from the Roman numerals of the front matter to the Arabic numbers of the main text. Final formatting includes a number of elements, including: front matter, headings/subheadings, margins, page numbers, tables, figures, references, and appendices.

The front matter consists of all the elements of text that appear before your first chapter. The APA manual—because it's designed more for article publication than dissertations—doesn't specify many of these elements, so you'll need to defer carefully to your university guidelines here. However, the front matter usually includes: title page, copyright page, signature page (where your committee members and advisor or other university leaders sign their approval), dedication, acknowledgments, abstract, table of contents, lists of tables and figures, and sometimes a list of acronyms.

There's no two ways about it, formatting can be a pain; however, here are some tips that can make it a little easier. Your future self will thank you!

- Carefully review your university submission guidelines. This cannot be understated. While you may have been told to "just follow APA," it's worth noting that most universities have their own idiosyncratic rules regarding margins, spacing, headings, and stuff like that. Some university guides are worse than others. There are several guides we've encountered that require the top margin on the first page of each chapter to be different than the top margin on every other page: a total unnecessary headache!
- If you've been given a template, use it! We constantly encounter students who have just written

their drafts on their own ignoring their university's template. This creates a lot more work later as you have to cut, paste, or otherwise shoehorn an existing document into a university-approved template. If you just start writing in the template from the beginning, your future self will thank you!

- Embrace MS Word Styles. Microsoft word has a feature that allows you to "style" different types of text. If you set up what "level 1" and "level 2" headings are supposed to look like in MS Word's styles and then apply those to your headings throughout your document, you'll be able to generate an automated table of contents. Lauren—who has now edited dissertations for a living for the past seven years—can vividly remember trying to create her table of contents manually. She'd type individual periods to get the page numbers to the right side of the page, rather than learning how to use a tab leader or the automated table of contents (they used to never line up). Worse, she inserted every page number manually, so she had to change each of them when she revised the text and the page numbers changed.

- Use styles with your table and figure titles. Just as the other heading levels will enable you to create an automated table of contents, using styles with your tables and figures will enable you to create automated lists of tables and lists of figures.

- Cite and reference meticulously throughout the writing process. This was mentioned earlier, but bears repeating. Cleaning up your references and citations at the very end of the process can be laborious.

If you've read the above tips and think, "oh crap I wish I'd done that" or, "oh no, what have I gotten myself into," remember that the final formatting is one of the easiest things you can outsource to a professional. Maybe you don't want to learn how to create and properly format automated tables of contents in Microsoft Word? There are certainly more interesting things to spend your time and energy on. Feel free to let someone else handle this part so you can focus your time and energy on the research you're developing.

When to Stop

As we've discussed throughout this text, there is a point at which perfectionism is the enemy of completion. It's important to put together a polished finished product, and imperative that it's a piece of writing that you are proud of and of which your advisor approves. However, you will never be 100 percent happy with every aspect of it. You'll regret some of the limitations to your research process and wish you could conduct parts of your study again. You'll still have a niggling feeling that you should have read one more book or article. You'll wonder if it's worth running your literature review terms through the library database again, in case new work has been published in the last couple of months. You'll wonder if there was a better way to make that point in Chapter 5. Oscar Wilde is reported to have said, after a long day of writing: "I spent the morning putting in a comma, and the afternoon taking it out again." If you've reached this stage of the process, your dissertation is PhDone. Now it's time to prepare for your defense.

Dissertation Defense Preparation

The time has come: your dissertation or thesis defense is looming. You've spent months, if not years, working on your dissertation or thesis, and the process is almost over. Your committee members will need to review a final draft of your dissertation prior to the defense date. How much advanced time they require will vary from one university to the next, so be sure to double check that. Some institutions will simply allow you to email your dissertation to your committee members, while others may require you to distribute hard copies. Schools may handle the specifics of a defense differently from each other, so it's important to find out exactly what is expected, what kinds of timelines you should anticipate, and what you need to do, but here are some general tips to help you prepare for your defense.

Know Your Audience

To make sure you prepare an effective defense, it is important that you know your committee well. Do your research on them. Know their areas of expertise, and plan accordingly. Read over the comments and feedback you've gotten and see how you've addressed any weaknesses or issues they've pointed out. Consider whether there are themes across the board in the comments from your readers about your dissertation. Do you know how these committee members generally act during a defense? What are they like in the classroom? Do you know anyone who had them on their committee? If you have an idea of what to expect, you can be better prepared for strong personalities, further questioning about comments they made before, or recurrent issues they have with topics in your work.

Attend Other Defenses

If you can attend dissertation defenses of others in your cohort, do it. You will get a sense of how defenses are run in your program, and you can take notes on what not to do and observe nervous habits to avoid. You'll see how other students use visual aids and PowerPoints, and how different kinds of presentations are received. Pay as much attention to the examiners as you do to the student to see how they react. What works? What doesn't? It will also reduce your fear of the unknown; you've already attended some defenses and have a better general idea of how the process will go for you.

Be Prepared

You cannot overprepare for this, but you certainly can underprepare. Practice your speech, go over your slides, go over any handouts you're passing out, reread your dissertation and the notes from your readers, and do it all over again once you're done. It's also important to be aware of the habits you have when you get nervous. When you practice, be mindful of how you handle stress (e.g., do you talk faster?). If so, make sure you remember to breathe and speak slowly. Otherwise, your voice will feel high and tight in your throat, which will make you feel like you're being strangled, and will make you more nervous. Remember to have a conversation with people you know and are rooting for you, however stern they might seem. For prep, ask a friend or family member to go through a trial run as your audience and ask you questions. Come up with questions you'd rather *not* be asked, and have answers prepared. At Dissertation Editor, we often provide defense coaching services in which we listen to your presentation and ask you questions as if we were on your committee. Going through the process ahead of time can make it feel much less intimidating.

Know That Anything Can and Will Happen

Even with the best preparation, the unexpected can happen. You might get some curveball questions or be challenged in ways you didn't anticipate. You might not immediately have an answer to a question. You might stumble over an explanation, or the PowerPoint might not work—you can't control everything. That's okay. Your preparation will help you get through it and allow you to focus on what you can control, and thus, move forward.

Act the Part

You're the expert. This is *your* work, your dissertation. You are an expert on what you've written. You should know it inside and out. Don't explain to the committee that you're exhausted or that you were unsure about something. Don't overdo the jargon, but do make sure to speak in a collected, knowledgeable, professional way. Dress appropriately as well—don't show up in jeans and a hoodie. The same "business casual" type attire you'd wear for a conference presentation or to teach a class would be appropriate here as well.

The Night Before

Get some sleep. You'll be nervous, yes. But don't underestimate how much sleep you'll need. It will help keep you focused and sharp, as well as help you emotionally.

Don't forget—this is all preparation for the defense, but also be prepared for revisions to your dissertation after the defense. This is perfectly normal, and most students have revisions to make. Above all else, don't panic. Even if you blank during the defense, have an attack of the nerves, or get a crippling migraine and feel like you're looking at your committee through a kaleidoscope, your committee is attending your defense with the intention of having a good academic conversation and they likely won't let you stop them from having it. While it is theoretically possible that you could fail your defense, it is highly unlikely. From a cynical but realistic perspective, your department gets a lot of heat from the administration to make sure that their pass rate is fairly high, otherwise, students would never bother with the school. And, like it or not, schools are businesses, and it's bad optics for them to fail too many students. So, if you make it to the defense, for all intents and purposes, you've made it. Then again, if you show up and don't make any sense during your defense, while you might begrudgingly get awarded the degree, don't expect glowing recommendation letters.

Enjoy Yourself

It may seem counter-intuitive because the name *defense* implies that you should be defensive and ready to defend against an attack, but it doesn't have to be this way. If you go into the defense with a tense, defensive mindset, then most likely that will be your experience. However, you can reframe the defense into a celebration.

For probably the first and last time, you will have the amazing opportunity to sit in a room with four or five brilliant scholars (your committee) who have all meticulously pored over your dissertation. No one is ever going to care about your scholarship this much again. Relish it.

No, seriously. If you look forward to the opportunity to pick the brains of these individuals to find out what their critiques of your work are and how the project might be improved, you have just created invaluable feedback that can drastically influence the way you approach future publications (books, journal articles, etc.) that are based on this same research. The defense is often the first time these scholars (your committee) will have all sat in the same room to think about your research. A comment from one of them may spur another one on to make a thought or suggestion that has never come up before. These epiphanies can only happen in the hallowed halls of the dissertation defense. This is a golden opportunity that students often miss because they are so fixated on the word defense that they enter the room defensively and fail to see the gift that this experience can be if they choose to allow it to be one.

Lastly, at most universities, you aren't allowed to defend your dissertation without first gaining the approval of your advisor. As a result, most advisors aren't going to feed their students to the wolves. Their own reputations are also at stake here. If your advisor feels like your dissertation is ready for defense, it probably is. There's no reason to panic. There's every reason to celebrate.

Lauren passed her dissertation defense with minor corrections (fairly substantial revisions to the introduction, but not much to change in the rest of the document) and was congratulated by her advisor and two committee members. Her outside committee member paused and said, "the best advice I can give you is to stay in this room for the next couple of hours taking notes before you go celebrate. The conversation we just had will help you with your final revisions, as well as with ideas for your future research." Lauren thought that was great advice in theory, but in practice she waited just long enough for her outside committee member to return to her office, then proceeded to the bar for celebratory drinks. She eventually made fairly detailed notes on topics covered during the defense, but the ideal best-of-both-worlds approach would likely be asking for permission to record the defense so that you're both free to celebrate immediately after it *and* equipped with a detailed record of a conversation that will provide great direction for your dissertation revision process and future work.

How to Create an Effective PowerPoint

Giving a PowerPoint presentation is often the opening salvo of the dissertation defense. It sets the tone for what is to follow. A well-done PowerPoint can be a powerful thing. It can engage a crowd, teach students, convey your hard-won research findings, and help disseminate knowledge. The line between a good PowerPoint and a bad one, however, is too often crossed. Many clients come to us for assistance with their thesis or dissertation PowerPoints, needing editing and reformatting because of negative feedback they've received. Here are some helpful tips on how you can construct an effective and engaging PowerPoint.

Focus on Substance, Not Style, at First

We've seen clients who are preoccupied with their clip art, pictures, memes, fonts, colors, and designs instead of the actual material on the slides—and this never makes for a strong presentation. Writing the text of your presentation is the first thing you should do, and until the text is revised and polished, don't even think about the aesthetics of the PowerPoint. That will come later—and, really, it wouldn't be the worst to give a presentation sans PowerPoint. Still, the most important aspect of a visual aid is getting your main points across in a clear and concise way.

Whatever You Do, Don't Read From the Slides!

If you have ever attended a horrible PowerPoint presentation, you will know that invariably it consists of someone reading aloud what is written on the screen. It's only slightly more interesting than watching paint dry or grass grow, and it seems to progress at the same pace. Instead, make notes for yourself on what you are going to say *while* your audience takes in an image, table, graph, or figure. If you must put an outline of what you plan to discuss on the slides, make it as brief as possible. Your audience wants to hear you speak and they can read so much faster than you can talk. If you tell them on the slide what you are about to say, you are, in effect, repeating yourself, which is what makes watching someone read a slide so boring.

Brevity Is the Soul of Wit

This old adage remains true, but it's also something to keep in mind with PowerPoint presentations. Cluttered slides full of text often cause audience members to zone out or simply not pay attention to you. A PowerPoint should highlight main ideas, not consist of everything you're going to say.

Size Matters . . . for Graphics

If you have graphs, charts, or visual representations of your data, make sure they are legible and easy to read. Same with text. So, avoid overloading slides, using hard-to-read fonts, including unnecessary images that don't add much, and using creative "formatting." See Figure 2 for an overly busy slide:

Figure 2
A Busy Slide

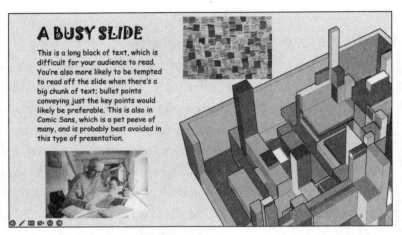

Make It Easy on the Eyes

Once you have written and edited the text, then you can focus on making it pretty. Choose pops of color and a visual theme, but don't go overboard. You don't want a rainbow of colors on slides to distract the audience from the message. Avoid clip art if you can and use stock images instead. Use animation *very* sparingly, if at all. When in doubt, go with simple, direct formats like bullet points or minimal text on the page, and align your text consistently.

Less Is More: Really

This one bears repeating because we see it all the time, over and over. Remember, *a PowerPoint presentation is a supplement to your presentation rather than the whole presentation.*

You shouldn't be reading from it; it should simply serve to reinforce the main concepts and points.

Final Revisions and Form and Style Review

As mentioned before, typically, final revisions are requested *after* a dissertation has been successfully defended. These can be minor things like missing citations or references, or they could be more substantial issues like elaborating on a particular idea or concept that one or more of your committee members felt was underdeveloped in your dissertation. Your advisor should not, at this stage, have any revisions for you to make as they should have approved your dissertation prior to the defense. However, your other committee members may raise issues or concerns that were not previously voiced by your advisor.

Fortunately, you do not have to defend your dissertation again once you have passed the defense. Some universities may ask you to submit your revised draft to your committee before they sign the signature page, while others may not. For the most part, it's up to you to make the necessary corrections prior to submitting your final draft to the University. Before you are allowed to upload your dissertation to ProQuest, your dissertation will still need to be checked by the University's form and style reviewer. This is typically someone in the University, often affiliated with the library, whose task is to ensure uniformity among all the dissertations submitted at the university in terms of formatting. They are the ones making sure that you followed the university guidelines for issues of spacing, page numbers, margins, headings, and appropriate usage of academic style. These types of revisions often require another close look at your university template or guidelines for small details you may have missed (like spacing, proper use of subheadings, or elements that are missing from your reference list, like DOIs). For more on this, see the earlier section on "Final Formatting" on page 159.

Submitting Your Dissertation to ProQuest

After your final revisions are complete, your manuscript has been edited, and you are finished with your thesis or dissertation, you'll usually be required to upload your manuscript to ProQuest. What is ProQuest, you might ask? ProQuest Central is the largest multidisciplinary full-text database on the market, providing access to 47 of ProQuest's databases, encompassing more than 175 subjects, making it one of the largest research resources in the world. Every year, more than 130,000 dissertations are added to ProQuest.

What's Involved in Submitting My Manuscript to ProQuest?

You can submit your dissertation or thesis to ProQuest in two ways: through the official online submission tool called ETD Administrator or through your school's electronic submission method, which they then submit to ProQuest. It is typically required that you submit your document in PDF format, so make sure all the formatting is correct and appropriate prior to final submission. It cannot be password protected and no digital signature should be on it. If you have any supplemental information—like spreadsheets, audio, or video—they need to be added as supplementary files and described in your abstract, along with any supporting documentation like reprint permission letters or third-party software licenses.

What About Embargo Options?

Students have the option to embargo their manuscripts for one or two years. You might choose the embargo option so you can submit articles to journals for publication, if there are any patents pending, or if you're concerned about data privacy. Some students want to turn their dissertation into a book, and an embargo may be a good choice if you're thinking about this. People will then need to buy your book to read your research rather than being able to look up your dissertation online for free through their institution. If you're planning to hold off until a new publication comes out, the longer the embargo the better. If you're considering putting an embargo on your manuscript, talking with your dissertation advisor about it can help you make an informed decision.

Will My Dissertation Be Copyrighted?

If you live in the United States and want to register a copyright for your dissertation, you can do this through the ETD Administrator in ProQuest by paying $55.00 to protect your manuscript and become immediately eligible for statutory damages and attorney fees. Copyright attaches at the time of creation, but registering for copyright makes it easier to sue should there be any infringement on your intellectual property. If you pay for the registration service, ProQuest submits the application to the United States Copyright for you and then gives you the certificate from the Library of Congress. Once your manuscript is published on ProQuest, a permanent link is created. This can be especially beneficial because it helps protect your work and your intellectual property.

Most importantly, congratulations are in order at this juncture, at which you have completed the gargantuan task of writing, finalizing, and editing your PhD! Before you do anything else, this is an important time to take a break, revisit some of the work-life balance questions discussed earlier and make time for celebration and rest. Lauren made the mistake of switching off a little too completely by removing her school email from her phone and missing an important deadline to register for spring graduation. She ended up unnecessarily waiting until summer. So, take some well-earned time to decompress, but be sure to set calendar reminders, etc., and stay on track with any institutional formalities you need to finalize the degree. After you've had a chance to recover and rebalance—and regain some objectivity regarding your manuscript—it's time to turn to the next chapter and consider the next steps you can take with your completed dissertation.

CHAPTER 8

Where Do You Go From Here?

Publishing Your Research

For most early career researchers interested in pursuing careers in academia, the dissertation becomes the first book they publish as a fully-fledged academic with a PhD. Importantly, the book is *based on* the dissertation, but it is not the dissertation itself. As mentioned previously, the audience of your dissertation is the five-person committee appointed to determine if you are worthy of receiving your degree or not. A dissertation is *not* a compelling medium for conveying your research to a broad and interested scholarly audience. For that, you'll need to write a book or a journal article, and there's a lot to consider in that process.

Turning your dissertation into a scholarly monograph, and publishing it with a university press, is one of the first steps in advancing your career as an academic, gaining a wider scholarly audience for your work, and beginning to build your portfolio for applying for promotion or tenure later in your career. Depending on your field and your dissertation, an article placed with a well-respected journal in your field might be an even more effective approach to establishing yourself as an expert in your dissertation's area of study.

Many doctoral graduates have no intention of pursuing careers in academia. However, without publishing their research in another format, they are ensuring that virtually no one will read it. How many dissertations had you read before starting graduate school? I'll be shocked if the answer isn't zero. Publishing your research establishes you as a thought-leader in your field. It creates prestige and notoriety that extends far beyond the letters at the end of your name. For many of our clients who seek out our Dissertation-to-Book conversion service, publishing a book is the first step toward launching a new business or new career. Don't let burnout at the end of the doctoral journey lead to wasted opportunities. Publish your research while it is still fresh and exciting.

My Book Is My Brand

Doctoral students should realize that their dissertations and subsequent publications brand them, for better or worse, and affect their futures. The dissertation and/or book title will appear near the top of their career vita and will make an impression on the reader. This is a feature of the work that may lead to alterations in their topic or their approach according to their career aspirations. Most importantly, choosing to publish your dissertation as a book or article is the moment this branding will most fully occur, and so it's an important time to consider changes you want to make to it, or particular parts of it you want to focus most on emphasizing.

Imelda, a doctoral candidate at Pepperdine, approached her advisor with a dissertation plan to study the complex identities of

Black women. This topic is sometimes labeled "intersectionality," emphasizing the identities of people who live at the intersection of two mostly visible identities. Imelda proposed an interview-based study to inquire into women's self-concept at this intersection. Most studies of this subject had used a qualitative approach, exploring Black women's identity by discovering themes in their discourse. Imelda wanted to continue in this tradition.

Imelda and her advisor talked, trying to shape the general idea into something dissertation-worthy that hadn't already been covered in the literature. "I want to take a different approach, maybe try to define various identity statuses more clearly in my interviews," Imelda said. Her advisor remembered, from having Imelda in classes, that she was unusually quick to grasp statistical principles and see how they apply to research methods. Also, Imelda was an ambitious student who wanted to establish herself in academia: "I want to be a name people know in my area of study." With this knowledge, the advisor suggested that Imelda try a statistical analysis to explore her research question. Maybe qualitative researchers had uncovered all there was to uncover, and it was time to establish quantitative evidence. Furthermore, given the values of prestigious departments at the time, writing a statistical dissertation would place Imelda ahead of other researchers in her area.

The two discussed multidimensional scaling, an approach that attempts to discover discrete groupings of subjects based on their similarities and differences in response to established scales—in this case, measures of Black identity status and women's identity status. Imelda hadn't learned multidimensional scaling in classes, but her advisor assured her that she could learn it and gave her some sample articles, and the two had tutorial meetings on the approach.

Imelda's analysis was a success—four distinct groups of Black women emerged: Black identity foremost, woman identity foremost, engaged mixed identity, and aware but not engaged mixed identity. Gendered racial identity among Black women was not a homogenous construct, as a common misconception claimed earlier. Aspects of Imelda's dissertation were quickly and smoothly accepted for publication in a major journal, and she became a notable and widely cited name in her field. Imelda started focusing on her brand at an early stage in the process, leading to great success in publishing.

Is My Dissertation a Book, an Article, or Both?

The first thing to consider is your field and the structure of your dissertation. If you conducted a study and submitted a five-chapter dissertation, it might lend itself well to becoming your first article. In the types of fields that tend to require a five-chapter dissertation (for example, education, psychology, sciences, business, and nursing), the ideal avenue for the publication of academic studies is top journals in the field. Such articles often contain the exact same sections as a dissertation (introduction, literature review, methodology, results, and discussion), so your article may be a (very) abridged version of your dissertation document. In humanities fields that have a more flexible dissertation format (literature, history, theatre, and some fine arts), the decision between article and book is often based on the amount of material already published on your subject, the structure of your dissertation, and the amount of material that will need to be added to it for it to function as a monograph. Lastly, you may want to consider the length of the dissertation you've written and the amount of material you have. Some disciplines allow for very short dissertations (80 to 120 pages). These dissertations are excellent candidates for articles due to their already somewhat abridged nature. Other disciplines require much longer dissertations, which would make them better candidates for converting into a book or into both a book and an article.

Time is another important factor to consider here. Revising and publishing an article is likely to take significantly less time than converting your dissertation into a scholarly monograph, so publishing one chapter as an article first, then moving forward with the book revision process, may allow you to get your ideas out there more quickly. If other researchers are working on similar topics, it's important to be mindful of not letting an inordinate amount of time pass before your book or article is published.

How to Convert Your Dissertation into a Book

As mentioned before, your dissertation is best understood as a very early rough draft of your first book. On book proposals for academic publishers, there is often a question asking whether the monograph is based on your dissertation and, if so, what substantial revisions you've already undertaken. Publishers want to see that you've made significant changes to take the text from dissertation to a book appropriate to their wider scholarly audience. Here are some tips on how to do it.

You Can't Submit Your Dissertation for Publication "As Is"

You are rightfully proud of the dissertation you produced and its acceptance by a group of your academic superiors. But a dissertation is never publisher-ready: that is, don't even try to send your unedited dissertation to a press. They will immediately reject it.

Dissertations tend to be narrower in focus than publishable books and often have stilted formats and language that must be revised for publication. This is not to denigrate the hard work that you have done, but rather to underscore that a first draft needs further revision. Unlike a dissertation, a book doesn't have to challenge existing paradigms as much as it has to contribute to a growing body of scholarship.

Heed the Criticisms of Your Dissertation Committee

Take advantage of the issues and potential problems raised in your dissertation defense. Your defense was a rare opportunity to present your work to a committee of experts exclusively focused on you and your ideas. Resist the urge to be defensive when you hear criticism of your dissertation. Graciously receiving the constructive criticism of other scholars will only make you better. During your defense, jot down your committee members' thoughts and eventually use them to make your book even better. If you are overwhelmed by this process, consider asking a good friend to attend your defense and take copious notes for you. If your defense is closed to the public, consider taking time after your defense to record your thoughts and notes on the issues raised before you forget them. Even if it's the last thing you want to do after a successful defense, these notes may prove invaluable to your future endeavors (and a little more time chilling is unlikely to hurt the champagne). It has already been mentioned in an earlier chapter that Lauren skipped this process to hit the bar. If you need a long exhale after this extremely stressful stage of your academic journey, then take it, take it immediately, and sort out the details later. Lastly, some institutions will allow you to make an audio recording of the proceedings. This shouldn't replace your notes, but it can be an effective tool for retrieving specific ideas and contributions from your faculty. The comments from your committee could generate the core of your new focus in the book to come.

Take a Break From Your Dissertation

You probably won't be tempted to do this anyway, but don't jump into your revisions immediately after you graduate. Give yourself some time to mull it all over (some people take years, we recommend several months). Ask yourself: What parts of my research or work did I enjoy the most? What turned out to be most compelling? What chapters worked and which ones need significantly more work?

Don't be afraid to cut chapters wholesale from your manuscript. Sometimes you have to start fresh, even if it means going back to the archives or pulling out your research again. Now that you are older and hopefully wiser, you will have fresh eyes and a new perspective. Take some time after graduation to relax, but also just to think about the dissertation and what it might look like as a book—don't rush into book mode. Think about what worked, what didn't, what you want to cut, and what you want to explore in more detail, now that you have the freedom to do so. Let ideas percolate and see what comes to the surface.

Appealing to a Wider Audience

You were writing your dissertation to please fewer than ten people; in contrast, a book must appeal to a larger and more diverse audience. For a publisher to accept the research and ideas present in your dissertation, you have to scale back on the academic jargon. If you haven't done so already, you need to develop a personal writing style that sets you apart and attracts the editors at the press you are targeting for publication. Your advisor or colleagues can be helpful in directing you toward the best fit for your subject matter and personal style.

Length is another important consideration when converting a dissertation into a book. Depending on your publisher's requirements, you may either need to expand the manuscript, or make cuts to it. You may need to remove those long and unwieldy footnotes—if applicable. Publishers will humor more established scholars and allow them to include 50–100 pages of notes and references, but for the rest of us, it is wise to include only the most relevant and important ones and to keep them short and to the point. Also, if you've quoted a lot of material from various primary and secondary sources, you will likely have to cut out a lot of it. Publishers will likely require you not to go over a set number of quoted words. Otherwise, they will have to pay the publishers of those works to reprint the various sections you've quoted. Similarly, if you used copywritten images or materials in your dissertation, you may need to seek additional permissions to use them in your publication.

Rethink Your Purpose

You had something to prove with the dissertation and needed to cite and cross-reference extensively to prove your knowledge and to prove that you read every possible book and article even remotely related to your topic. In a book, you don't need to do that as much (although you do cite when necessary). It is assumed you're knowledgeable about the subject—that's why you're writing the book. Take another look at your topic and your objective with fresh eyes. What might be changing as it turns into a book?

Cut It Out

All that clunky, academic jargon? Rewrite it into more conversational, yet smart language. You want people to be able to read and enjoy your work, and the jargon isn't necessary. It's likely that you'll need to cut a lot of the cross-referencing, data, and footnotes, or at least incorporate much of it into your actual text, if you keep it.

Find Your Voice

You've been in school for so long, and, with the dissertation, were at the mercy of your committee, with multiple people to please. This can result in a lack of voice on the page. Take the time to find your voice and writing style. Do some free writing or journaling. Write some op-eds or response pieces, even if they're for your eyes only. Write about something you love or find interesting and ask others to read it and provide feedback. The voice on the page can make or break a book, no matter how fascinating the subject is—if there's no voice, there's no book. Some great books to help you find your writing voice include *On Writing Well: The Classic Guide to Writing Nonfiction* by William Zinsser; and *The Artist's Way* by Julia Cameron. Don't let the last one scare you off—it's wonderful for writer's block and developing your style and voice. Also, take a look at the monographs of others you admire. How did they turn their dissertations into books? With ProQuest, you can read the "before and after" to see just what they did.

Converting Your Dissertation (Or Part of It) Into a Journal Article

After spending years of your life on a dissertation, it's important for it to see the light of day. As mentioned in the previous section on converting it into a book, no one reads dissertations. But you'd like to have people read your research, right? For a broader public audience, a book is perhaps the best bet in terms of prestige, accessibility, and, of course, getting paid when people purchase it. Be warned, the book royalties on the average academic monograph won't go very far to buying that chateau in Nice that you've had your eye on. Though not even providing the meager royalties of an academic book, a journal article can be a great addition to your publication strategy.

Placing your research in an academic journal gives you the credibility of having had your work accepted by a venue that vets its contributions through a peer-review process. It also puts your research into the hands of the people who are likely to care about it the most—other scholars in your field. If you are planning to pursue a career in academia, publishing journal articles is an absolute must. Even if your career path is taking you elsewhere, establishing yourself as a recognized thought leader in your field through journal publication is definitely a feather in your cap.

A journal article is also a great complement to a book—especially if you are self-publishing. The journal article isn't nearly as long and only provides the readers with one facet of your research. If they want the whole story, then they need to buy the book!

Lastly, a journal article is a much easier project than a book conversion, simply because it isn't that long. Journal articles range from 3,000 to 10,000 words (twelve to forty pages) depending on the journal. Whereas a full book manuscript is a much larger (and more involved) project.

How to Create a Journal Article From Your Dissertation

The first thing to consider when creating a journal article is the target journal. Where are you planning to submit your article? Obviously, the first place to look is the flagship journals of your field. Undoubtedly, a handful should immediately come to mind. Beyond that, review your own reference list. Where are the articles you cited in your research published? Would one of those journals make a good home for your article?

Selecting the journal goes hand-in-hand with selecting the argument from your research that you wish to present. You aren't going to share the entire research project in one article, but rather are going to select an important aspect of your work for publication. As you think about your subtopic, you'll also think about your target journal. Ideally, it will be an obvious connection between your target journal and the general thrust of your argument. That will be the best recipe for acceptance.

Drafting the Article

Much like every other type of academic writing, you will be well served by extensively outlining your argument before you start writing. This will help you organize your ideas and get a sense of the trajectory of the entire article *before* you sit down in front of the blank screen of death. Since you are basically reshaping material you have already researched, you should know about the topic already. It's just a matter of selecting what to exclude—which is easier said than done. For that reason, instead of trying to cut your dissertation down to an article, we recommend creating an outline for the article first, deciding what you are going to include, and then slowly adding that material until you have developed the article in its entirety. It is unlikely that you will cut and paste much from your dissertation. More often, you will rewrite that material as it will need to be said differently in this shorter format. Another tip would be to outline some articles from the target journal and then modify those outlines to fit your material.

Once you have drafted the article, edit it, revise it, and have it proofread by friends or professionals. Double check that you have followed the submission guidelines to the "t". When it is time to submit the article, you want to be sure that you are making the best first impression possible. The last thing you want is for your article to be rejected due to issues with grammar or formatting. And such rejections are all too common with journals. When editors see formatting errors, they will often reject an essay without even reading it.

What Do I Do If My Article Is Rejected?

First, take a deep breath. Second, take another deep breath for good measure. This is not the end of the world and does not mean that you have conducted poor scholarship. It probably means that this research simply wasn't meant for that journal. Allen's first article was rejected. He sent it to a second-tier journal because he was hoping for an easy win. When he got the news, he was devastated for a couple of weeks, until a friend told him to make a few tweaks and send it to a different journal—just to see what would happen. Sure enough, the same article was accepted by the flagship journal in Allen's field. A year or so later, that article won an award at a national conference for its contribution to the field. When an article gets rejected, it could be for any number of reasons, including, but not limited to, what the editor had for lunch that day and how well he or she slept the night before reading your draft. Whatever you do, don't despair.

As mentioned earlier, a rejection from one journal often comes with advice for revising and improving your draft before submitting it elsewhere. Revision is key to producing good scholarship. The next time you submit your article, it will be better. That still doesn't mean it will get accepted. However, if you have fully addressed the feedback you received on the first submission, then the odds are in your favor.

Conclusion: PhDone

A dissertation is a singular experience. There's nothing quite like it, and completing it admits you to membership in an eclectic but smart circle of fellow doctors. Whether you choose to stay in academia, using your hard-earned wisdom to shepherd future doctoral candidates through the dissertation process as an advisor, or apply your skills in a different field, completing a dissertation is a point of pride and an extreme sort of academic exercise that will refine your thinking and communicating, giving you a new and enduring professional edge.

Not only does it entitle you to the title of doctor and status as a *world expert* in your area of study, but it also equips you with skills that will remain with you for the rest of your career and life. You can use the writing strategies you fine-tuned during the process of drafting your dissertation when you write your next several books or articles. You can apply your research skills to your role with a nonprofit, turning up grants none of your colleagues had even heard of. You can navigate challenges with the knowledge that—given the right preparation, and the insight of those who have undertaken the process before you—you are more than capable of competing with them. Writing a dissertation is a long and difficult process, but if you are determined, then nothing can stop you from completing your goal. You can be PhDone.

References

American Psychological Association. (2020). *The publication manual of the American Psychological Association* (7th ed.). https://doi.org/10.1037/0000165-000

Booth, W. C., Colomb, G. G., Williams, J. M., Bizup, J., & FitzGerald, W. T. (2016). *The craft of research* (4th ed.). The University of Chicago Press.

Cameron, J. (2016). *The Artist's Way*. Tarcher Perigee.

Eco, U. (2015). *How to write a thesis* (C. M. Farina & Geoff Farina, trans.). MIT Press. (Original work published 1977).

Elbow, P. (2012). *Vernacular eloquence: What speech can bring to writing*. Oxford University Press.

Goodwin, D. (1987). *The Fitzgeralds and the Kennedys*. Simon and Schuster.

Graff, G., & Birkenstein, C. (2014). *"They say / I say": The moves that matter in academic writing* (3rd ed.). W.W. Norton & Company.

Kirkpatrick, D. D. (2002a, January 5). 2 say Stephen Ambrose, popular historian, copied passages. *The New York Times*. https://www.nytimes.com/2002/01/05/us/2-say-stephen-ambrose-popular-historian-copied-passages.html

Kirkpatrick, D. D. (2002b, June 5). Author Goodwin resigns from Pulitzer board. *The New York Times.* https://www.nytimes.com/2002/06/01/us/author-goodwin-resigns-from-pulitzer-board.html

Lamott, A. (1995). *Bird by bird: Some instructions on writing and life* (1st Anchor Books ed.). Anchor Books.

O'Conner, P. T. (2009). *Woe Is I: The grammarphobe's guide to better English in plain English* (3rd ed.). Riverhead Books.

Rabiner, S. (2003). *Thinking like your editor: How to write great serious nonfiction and get it published.* Norton.

Silvia, P. J. (2019). *How to write a lot: A practical guide to productive academic writing* (2nd ed.). American Psychological Association.

Strunk, W., White, E. B., & Elwyn B. (2000). *The elements of style* (4th ed.). Allyn and Bacon.

Zinsser, W. K. (1998). *On writing well: the classic guide to writing nonfiction* (6th ed.). HarperCollins.